THE GOSPEL ACCORDING TO ST. JOHN

NEW TESTAMENT FOR SPIRITUAL READING

VOLUME 9

Edited by

John L. McKenzie, S.J.

THE GOSPEL
ACCORDING TO ST. JOHN

Volume 3

Josef Blank

CROSSROAD · NEW YORK

1981
The Crossroad Publishing Company
575 Lexington Avenue, New York, NY 10022

Originally published as *Das Evangelium nach Johannes 3*
© 1977 by Patmos-Verlag
from the series *Geistliche Schriftlesung*
edited by Wolfgang Trilling
with Karl Hermann Schelke and Heinz Schürmann

English translation © 1981 by The Crossroad Publishing Company
Translated by Matthew J. O'Connell

Library of Congress Catalog Card Number: 81-68180
ISBN: 0-8245-0118-7

OUTLINE

INTRODUCTION

Lord, our Ruler,
whose name is glorious in every land!
Show us, through your passion,
that you, true Son of God,
have been glorified
at every moment,
even in deepest humiliation.

(J. S. Bach, *Passion according to John*)

The special character of the Johannine passion narrative requires that we approach it differently than we did the farewell discourses. Since the text of John is itself a meditation on the trial and execution of Jesus, we shall dispense with a separate meditation after our exegesis. The subject of the narrative is the central content of the New Testament message.

1. The passage cited above from the opening chorus of J. S. Bach's *Passion according to John* gives lapidary and fully correct expression to the theological aim of the Johannine passion narrative. The evangelist's purpose is in fact to show Jesus as glorified "even in deepest humiliation." John's account of the passion, taken as a whole, is hardly to be described as an account of the bitter suffering and death of Jesus, but is rather an account of the victory of Jesus! The cantor of St. Thomas' Church in Leipzig grasped this fully, as he shows, when, at the climactic moment between the final words of Jesus, "It is completed," and the evangelist's own words, "and he bowed his head and died," he introduces an aria which is a meditation on "It is completed" and closes with the words, "The hero from Judah conquers mightily, and ends the struggle; it is completed."

The Johannine Jesus is not the sacrificial victim of cruel inhuman circumstance. Neither is he, as in the passion according to Mark, the "suffering just man." He is rather the royal, messianic conquerer, and this from the very beginning of the passion. From the

3

moment Jesus is arrested, the reader of the Johannine account knows who, and who alone, is determining the entire course of events. It is Jesus who retains the initiative from beginning to end. In John's portrayal Jesus goes to his death freely and as one in sovereign control. It is not individuals, however important the part they play in the events, who hand Jesus over for crucifixion. What Jesus says to Pilate holds strictly for all the individuals and groups who take part in these proceedings of the unbelieving world against Jesus: "You would have no power over me if it were not given to you from above" (19:11). They could take no effective action against Jesus if power over him were not given to them from above, that is, by the divine word.

It is exclusively his obedience to the Father's will that causes Jesus to enter upon his way of suffering. This profound consent to the divine will—"My food is to do the will of him who sent me and bring his work to completion" (4:34)—which according to John marks the entire personality of Jesus, is, when seen from the other side, the sovereign freedom which Jesus manifests in his conduct. Consequently, nowhere in John does the superiority of Jesus to the world show itself so completely as in the passion story.

> This "bringer of glad tidings" dies as he lived, as he *taught*— *not* to "redeem mankind" but to demonstrate how one ought to live. What he bequeathed to mankind is his *practice*: his bearing before the judges, before the guards, before the accusers and every kind of calumny and mockery—his bearing on the *Cross*. He does not resist, he does not defend his rights, he takes no steps to avert the worst that can happen to him—more, he *provokes it.* . . . And he entreats, he suffers, he loves *with* those, *in* those who are doing evil to him. His words to the *thief* on the cross contain the whole Evangel. "That was verily a *divine* man, a child of God!"—says the thief. "If thou feelest this"—answers the redeemer—"*thou art in Paradise*, thou art a child of God." *Not* to defend oneself, *not* to grow angry, *not* to make responsible. . . . But not to resist even the evil man—to *love* him. . . . [1]

If we compare the Johannine passion narrative with that of Mark (Matthew and Luke both depend on Mark), we are struck chiefly by the fact that John represents *a different theological conception*

4

of the passion. This divergence is even emphasized inasmuch as the Markan and Johannine presentations are at one in many details and similar in their general outline. For this outline we can, with C. H. Dodd, distinguish five acts: Act I: The leave-taking (last supper, etc.); Act II: The arrest; Act III: The trial (Scene 1: Before the high priest; Scene 2: Before Pilate); Act IV: The execution; Act V: The reunion (burial; discovery of the empty tomb; the risen Jesus).[2] This arrangement gives us a good idea of the structure of the passion narrative, although the outline evidently does not take into account a whole series of variations, additions, etc.

If we look more closely at the various "acts" and their presentation in Mark and John, the differences emerge very clearly. John has taken the tradition he inherited concerning the suffering and death of Jesus, and has radically recast it. And it is theological viewpoints that chiefly determine the refashioning.

> It is typical of the fourth evangelist's understanding of the passion that he interprets the suffering and death as an exaltation and glorification of Jesus and a judgment on the world and its rulers. Jesus did not have to wait for his resurrection and exaltation to the Father's right hand in order to be vindicated by the Father; his passion itself is already illumined by the rays of Easter glory. Thus the account begins directly with an "epiphany miracle" that strikes the guards to the ground. The disciples owe their being let go free not to cowardly flight but to the powerful intervention of Jesus. Before the high priest the Lord shows himself the superior; his refusal to answer points ahead to the final judgment on the world. Most of all, however, it is the trial before Pilate (down to and including the dispute about the "title" or inscription on the cross) that highlights his majesty and the judgment of destruction that is being passed on the world. Finally, Jesus dies with the victorious words, "It is completed," on his lips. Even the events surrounding his burial speak of his glorification: God preserves his Son from further affronts and even makes him a sign to which all must raise their eyes.[3]

For this reason, any interpretation that is to do justice to the Johannine passion narrative must be concerned first and foremost with its theological statements and basic ideas. John has undoubtedly

5

incorporated traditional elements, including historical ones, into his new drama of the passion,[4] but the emphasis is not on these. It is rather on what John has done with these elements. This evangelist was a great creative artist and is not to be comprehended by means of dry philological erudition alone. That is why Bach's *Passion according to John* is not simply an artistic ecclesiastical reproduction of the story but a satisfactory interpretation of the text in the medium of music; it is exegesis in the strict sense of the word and, in its own terms as a work of art, it presents decisive moments and scenes of the Johannine text in a way that scholarly exegesis rarely succeeds.

The Johannine passion story, unlike the great revelatory and farewell discourses of this gospel, is unusually fast-paced. In manner of expression it is generally quite succinct; there are hardly any passages of complex detail. We receive the impression that the evangelist is trying to get through the entire story without delay and as quickly as possible. Any expansion by comparison with the synoptic tradition is to be seen chiefly in the trial before Pilate, which in terms of the material represents the internal climax of the passion according to John. But this very expansion has meant a gain in expressive power due to John's reworking of the material and his dramatization of both the outward events and the inner feelings of the participants.

In general, great care is shown in setting down statement after statement. John is a master of the art of epic terseness. Here is an example: the scene involving Barabbas takes only two verses in John (18:39-40; Mark uses ten verses, 15:6-15). The facts are condensed, and the verses give only Pilate's question and the people's answer, "Not this man but Barabbas!" which is followed by the crushing retort, "Now Barabbas was a murderer." In Mark we are told, "But Pilate wanted to placate the people, and he released Barabbas to them; then, having had Jesus scourged, he handed him over to the soldiers to be crucified" (15:13). Luke goes into even greater detail: "But Pilate decided to give them what they asked; he released the one they asked for who had been imprisoned for riot and murder, and he delivered Jesus to their will" (23:24-25). A glance at these various passages shows how much more forceful John's writing is here than that of Mark or Luke. It is so concentrated on a single point that it illumines as with a lightning flash the entire absurdity of the scene. This is what I mean by epic terseness. A number of

6

other examples could be given; the detailed exegesis will call attention to them.

A further characteristic is John's use of the device of role exchange. We have already mentioned that in the passion according to John Jesus alone dominates the stage throughout, despite the fact that he is a prisoner and will be executed in the end. Everyone else— the chief priests, Pilate, the Jews, even the soldiers of the execution squad—acts in accordance with another's will that is hidden and completely unknown to them. Whether or not they realize it, they fulfill a divine plan as though they were puppets. They have no inkling of all this; on the contrary, all of them think they are in the forefront as the ones controlling events, and indeed they are extremely active in bringing about the death of Jesus. On the surface, Jesus is the passive object of their activity and is being forced to submit to whatever they do to him. On the surface, in appearance, that is the way things seem to be: the active agents are the high priest, the Jews, Pilate, the soldiers, etc.; the passive one is Jesus. But in reality, if we look beyond appearances, the exact opposite is the case, and it is this interplay of appearance and reality that shapes John's presentation throughout.

All this is not merely a theological idea in John. Rather it is his special achievement to have taken the tension present in this kind of role exchange and to have turned it into a literary device for presenting the story. It is precisely this that creates the dramatic element in his passion narrative. In his *Passion according to John* Bach seized upon this point with special clarity and made good use of it. John "shows" (in Brecht's sense of the word) this drama; he brings it out, and for that reason (we want to emphasize this point again, since the professional theologians usually miss it completely) he is a great artist, a creative writer with a feel for meaningful effects, and not a mere theologian. The element of creativity and dramatic showing plays an absolutely decisive role in the passion as told by John. The continuous interaction of these complex relationships has totally pervaded the evangelist's literary production, but most clearly in the trial before Pilate (18:28–19:16).

In the course of such a presentation the individual scenes and especially a number of seemingly insignificant words and secondary features acquire a double meaning that at times borders on the eerie and reveals the hidden abyss in a person and in human relationships.

7

In 19:15, for example, the Jews say, "We have no king but Caesar," and thereby, in John's view, deny their own messianic hope for the sake of winning favor from an earthly ruler; every word here is deeply meaningful. Apparently external and secondary circumstances also acquire an unexpected importance: for example, indications of date and time of day, of locality, and so on. Thus the indecisiveness of Pilate in the trial of Jesus is brought out by the fact that the procurator is forced to go back and forth between the Jews outside in front of the residence and Jesus within it. By means of such stylistic devices the traditional material has been compressed and at the same time given new dimensions of meaning, while the Johannine passion narrative gives it an elevated literary expression.

We have begun by speaking in general terms of John's organization of the passion account; we have described it as compressed and as highly dramatized. We have thus been already making it clear that we are not dealing with a historical account of the trial and execution of Jesus, although it is beyond question that the Johannine passion story, like those of the other evangelists, has a historical basis of factual detail. The chief interest of the Johannine presentation lies in the fact that it elaborates the religious and theological background of meaning behind the arrest, trial, and execution of Jesus, and does so from the special viewpoint of this evangelist. It seems important, therefore, to give some particular attention to two questions: the first is the question of the historical basis or historical facts presupposed by the passion story; the second is the question of what John regards as the decisive reason for the execution of Jesus.

2. *The Historical Problem of the Trial and Execution of Jesus.* The fact that Jesus of Nazareth was executed on a cross is among those that are historically the most certain in the story of Jesus. But the exact date of Jesus' death can be ascertained only with probability; we have already discussed this point in the introduction to the farewell discourses (see vol. 2). We simply remind the reader that according to John the Friday on which Jesus was executed was the day of preparation for the Passover feast and therefore the fourteenth of Nisan, and that this dating is more probable than that of the synoptic writers (for whom Good Friday was the fifteenth of Nisan or the feastday of Passover).

8

Crucifixion was a Roman method of execution. It probably originated with the Persians and then became widespread in the Hellenistic and Roman periods. The Romans used it chiefly for slaves and rebels (among subject peoples); a Roman citizen could not be crucified but was beheaded. Apart from its cruelty, this method of execution was also a manifestation of special discrimination. The Jewish historian Flavius Josephus occasionally reports mass crucifixions. Thus the Hasmonean king Alexander Jannaeus (103-76 B.C.) once had eight hundred Jewish men, probably Pharisees, crucified at Jerusalem, and then, while they were hanging still alive on their crosses, had their wives and children slaughtered before their eyes; he himself meanwhile feasted with his harem and watched the execution.[5] During the disturbances that arose after the death of Herod the Great (Herod I) in the year 4 B.C., Varus had two thousand Jews crucified.[6]

It follows—and this is confirmed by the gospels—that Jesus was condemned to death by a Roman tribunal, in this case the tribunal of the procurator Pontius Pilate (in office A.D. 26-36), and executed as a rebel against Roman authority. According to the gospels the accusation was that Jesus was an aspirant to messiahship, that is, he sought to be "king of the Jews" (cf. Mark 15:2, 9, 12, 18; Matt. 27:11, 29; Luke 23:2, 3).

Jesus was brought before Pilate as an messianic pretender. The difficult question of whether Jesus had in fact claimed to be Messiah and, if he had, what precisely we are to understand by the claim, cannot be discussed in detail here.[7] We must start with the position that, given the contemporary situation, any messianic claim could only have been interpreted as a political claim. Josephus tells us of a series of individuals who were messianic aspirants[8] and whose pretensions to power were entirely political. Jesus himself, however, according to all that the gospels tell us, clearly separated himself from the political messianism of the day.

"The Gospel witness does not offer incontestable proof of the Messianic consciousness of Jesus. . . . The earliest tradition seems to present Jesus as an exorcist and healer, a prophet and teacher of wisdom, although with an authority which far surpasses that of any past prophets or teachers, Matthew 12:41f. par., and which grants him liberating power in the face of the might of evil, Mark 3:27." For "the title [of Messiah] as then understood was inadequate

9

to express His authoritative work."[9] According to the gospels it is always other people who take Jesus to be Messiah or Son of David, and these assertions prove over and over again to be problematic and subject to very serious misunderstandings.

Thus we are left with a difficulty: "Jesus was crucified as a Messianic pretender. The question of His Messiahship is thus at issue."[10] The question that needs answering, then, is this, how did the accusation against Jesus as king of the Jews arise? As a political accusation it was doubtless a misunderstanding. But there must have been reasons for the misunderstanding!

Are there any leads that will render the fate of Jesus more comprehensible in human and historical terms? Jesus was crucified as a rebel, but was he really guilty of any crime against the imperial Roman government? The thesis that he was in fact a political agitator, perhaps even a guerilla leader in the manner of the Jewish Zealots or freedom fighters, has often been proposed.[11] According to Pinchas Lapide, "Jesus of Nazareth was fully in the camp of the patriots in the Jewish resistance."[12] But the best of good will cannot make this a defensible thesis. The entry of Jesus into Jerusalem (Mark 11:1-10 par.; John 12:12-19) was rather a counterdemonstration against political messianism, and the significance of the cleansing of the temple (Mark 11:15-19 par.; John 2:12-17) was religious and eschatological, not political. And yet from a certain point of view it is possible to say that the political, social, and religious circumstances of contemporary Palestine combined to bring Jesus to his death.

The New Testament contains a very important parallel to Jesus: the person of John the Baptist. The evangelist and the early Church realized the parallel and referred to it expressly. The term "handed over" in Mark 1:14 ("After John had been handed over, Jesus came into Galilee") is evidently intended to point to the parallel destinies of the two prophets. The imprisonment and execution of the Baptist are narrated in detail.[13] The tradition even records the notion that John the Baptist had risen from the dead,[14] although this is presented as a superstition peculiar to Herod Antipas.

In this regard a notice in Flavius Josephus is especially enlightening:

Since the people were gathering in great numbers and being extraordinarily struck by his [John the Baptist's] words, Herod grew fearful that the man's eloquence might stir the

10

people to revolt, since they followed his advice in all matters. Herod regarded it as by far the most prudent thing to remove him from the scene in good time, before some unforeseen turn of events might occur, rather than to be forced to rue it later on after a dangerous upheaval. Because of these suspicions of Herod John was sent a prisoner to the fortress of Machaerus, which was mentioned earlier, and executed there.[15]

According to this account, Herod Antipas, the sovereign of Jesus and the Baptist, since both were Galileans, had the Baptist executed because he feared that John's activity might lead to an uprising. The Baptist and the mass movement he was provoking seemed politically dangerous to the king, or at least capable of being such, although, as Josephus himself insists, the movement was in no sense political. Fear of mass uprisings and demonstrations was abroad at that time in Palestine and especially in Judea, and was a good reason for taking steps against anyone who might possibly cause them; it made no difference whether the movement in question was genuinely religious or combined the religious and the political. We should not automatically credit the Roman authorities with the ability to make fine distinctions between a peaceful religious movement and a political uprising determined on using violence. In fact, it is incredible how completely lacking in understanding the Roman procurators were when it came to the Jewish religious situation. In the Roman view, religious movements and political movements alike endangered public order, especially since there was no telling when the former might suddenly turn into the latter.

The fate of the Baptist sheds some light on the fate of Jesus. Jesus had himself been initially a disciple of the Baptist and was undoubtedly very well informed about everything touching him. It did not require supernatural knowledge but only an unerring eye for the real facts, for Jesus to be able to anticipate what the future held for him, at least as an outside possibility. If by his preaching he were to create anything even faintly resembling a mass movement or a demonstration, then he would have to allow for the possibility of a violent death, for the reasons already given. The political situation of the day was such that a person like Jesus would be seen as a danger to public security by the dominant circles in Judaism and

11

by the Roman procurator. Against this background we can see how the charge of king of the Jews and messianic aspirant came to be made.

In the Roman view, religio-political troublemakers, such as the Zealots and their sympathizers, were rebels against Roman power and had to be eliminated; "brigands" or "criminals" was the official name for them. Now these same circles were the chief representatives of political messianism. If some wanted to get rid of Jesus, a legal argument was needed that would convince the Roman procurator, but this argument could be created simply by lumping Jesus and his movement together with the freedom movement of the Zealots. Pilate could not but understand the idea that someone was politically dangerous; the slogan, "king of the Jews," was eminently suited for making him think along these lines. Consequently Jesus was handed over to the procurator as a person accused of pretensions to a political messiahship.

We hardly need think of the accusation as an outright lie or a trick played on Pilate by the Jewish authorities. A messianic pretender could be someone bent on causing a violent upheaval; Barrabas the brigand who is mentioned as a rival of Jesus (Mark 15:6-14 par.; John 18:39-40) was probably such a person. But he could just as well be one of the harmless fanatics who in their idle talk proclaimed to the masses the miracles of the imminent era of salvation. The supreme council may well have put Jesus into the second group.

In any event, according to the passion narrative, the idea of "king of the Jews" provides the main accusation at the trial before Pilate, so that there can hardly be any doubt that this accusation was indeed made. Jesus himself had never made any such claim, but, as we have been saying, it seemed natural to see him as fitting this very dangerous pattern. Consequently, the spiritual and political authorities joined forces and crucified him as a rebel and "king of the Jews." This historical fact was a primary contributing factor in making Jesus of Nazareth the Messiah. In the New Testamental and early Christian understanding of the term the traditional Jewish concept of Messiah was, of course, radically transformed. The New Testament maintained the distinction between Jesus and any political Messiah.

In this connection there is another important point to be made. In an essay, "Jesus and the Sadducees,"[16] Karl-Heinz Müller has once again raised the question, "To which group among the contemporary Jewish religious parties did the real enemies of Jesus belong?"[17] His study concludes that the real enemies of Jesus were not the Pharisees but the Sadducees, the group comprising the temple aristocracy of chief priests. The Sadducees were concerned about the maintenance of the status quo, that is, the maintenance, above all, of the Jewish temple-state and its cultic order. Jesus' cleansing of the temple and his criticism of it must therefore have caused the Sadducean authorities, who held most of the seats in the supreme council, to intervene on the grounds that the sacred order seemed threatened. Müller says, "It is now clear why the synoptic account of the cleansing of the temple is placed at the beginning of the passion of Jesus; why the Sadducean priestly aristocracy plays the decisive role in eliminating Jesus; and why, finally, the Romans act as the agents who carry out the determination of this leading Jewish group to put Jesus to death."[18]

Müller also calls attention to a significant passage in Flavius Josephus that until now has hardly been given the importance due it in the discussion:

> An incident more alarming still had occurred four years before the war at a time of exceptional peace and prosperity for the City. One Jeshua son of Ananias, a very ordinary yokel, came to the feast at which every Jew is expected to set up a tabernacle for God. As he stood in the Temple he suddenly began to shout, "A voice from the east, a voice from the west, a voice from the four winds, a voice against Jerusalem and the Sanctuary, a voice against bridegrooms and brides, a voice against the whole people." Day and night he uttered this cry as he went through all the streets. Some of the more prominent citizens, very annoyed at these ominous words, laid hold of the fellow and beat him savagely. Without saying a word in his own defence or for the private information of his persecutors, he persisted in shouting the same. The Jewish authorities, rightly concluding that some supernatural force was responsible for the man's behaviour, took him before the Roman procurator. There, though scourged till his flesh hung in ribbons, he neither begged for mercy nor shed a tear, but lowering his voice to the most mournful of tones answered every blow with

13

"Woe to Jerusalem!" When Albinus—for that was the procurator's name—demanded to know who he was, where he came from and why he uttered such cries, he made no reply whatever to the questions but endlessly repeated his lament over the City, till Albinus decided he was a madman and released him. [19]

The parallels between this story and the New Testament accounts of the passion are surprising—arrest by the Jewish authorities, the prominent men (members therefore of the Sadducean party), the handing over to the Roman procurator, Albinus, the interrogation, the scourging—yet any dependence of the evangelists on Josephus is excluded, as is any dependence of Josephus on the evangelists. Still there is an essential difference between the two accounts: Albinus the procurator regards the man as mad and lets him go, whereas Pilate condemns Jesus to death. On this point Müller says:

> The prophecy of Jeshua son of Ananias proclaimed the destruction of the temple and the city. It was a direct hit at the group of "prominent citizens" in power at the time, the Sadducees, who had ideological and existential links with the temple. This group reacted irritably and with surprising harshness. The steps they took warrant close and detailed attention, since what we see in them is evidently a set sequence of judicial proceedings: the Sadducean aristocracy lay violent hands on the prophet of doom, interrogate him while beating him, and finally hand him over to the procurator who has the offender scourged and likewise subjects him to an official inquiry. The surrender of the man to the Romans certainly had a solely political motive: the Sadducees understood the prophecy of doom, so critical of the temple, as a declaration of war against the present order of things in the temple as well as a rejection of the power structure which the Romans had established and the Sadducean chief priests now represented. [20]

This text of Josephus thus confirms the historical credibility of the trial of Jesus in its basic components. Of course, in the gospels these components are set within the broader framework of a faith-inspired interpretation on the part of the evangelists.

The considerations Heinz Schürmann offers in his recent book *Jesu ureigener Tod* moves along the same lines. He asks, "In what manner did Jesus go to his death? How did he understand it?" It will hardly be disputed that Jesus could have grasped the danger inherent in his situation. In view of his execution by the Romans as a Zealot leader Schürmann says:

> Political misinterpretations of his activity were by no means impossible in a Galilean world that was thrown into a state of profound unrest by the political freedom fighters. . . . In particular, this misunderstanding cannot be excluded if the tradition is right in saying that Jesus accepted some former Zealots and Daggermen (*Sicarii*) into the circle of the Twelve; cf. "Simon the Zealot" (Luke 6:15 par.; Acts 1:13). It may be that we should regard "Judas Iscariot" too (Luke 6:15 par.; Acts 1:13) as a former Daggerman and interpret his behavior in the light of this fact.[21]

Schürmann sees in the disputes of Jesus with the two authoritative groups in Judaism, the Sadducees and the Pharisees, another important reason for his violent end. Like Müller, Schürmann believes that "we can say with reasonable certainty that it was the Sadducean priestly aristocracy which finally arranged for Jesus to be handed over to the Romans;[22] we should not, however, on that account dismiss "a growing opposition to Pharisaism."[23]

Two factors are especially important according to Schürmann. First, there is the radicalism of Jesus in his interpretation of God's will: "We are on historically sure ground when we see in Jesus' activity and preaching *an interpretation of God's will* that was so radical in its emphasis on God's holiness as to involve a rejection both of the Pharisaic interpretation of the Law and of Sadducean cult-centered piety."[24] The second factor was Jesus' solidarity with sinners: "We are likewise on sure ground when we emphasize *the solidarity of Jesus with sinners.*"[25] From all this Schürmann concludes, "Jesus' death was thus a consequence of his activity; in the last analysis it is to be explained by the interplay of several factors which even separately were always a source of danger to him."[26] On this point there is widespread agreement among exegetes today.

3. *What does John regard as the decisive reason for the execution of Jesus?* Modern exegetes were not the first to raise the question of the reasons and occasions for the violent death of Jesus. This had already been a matter of concern to the primitive Church and the

evangelists. Along with references to the Scriptures and to God's will we find an inquiry into the human causes at work and the reflection that the death of Jesus on the cross was not an accident but the consequence of his entire activity. Thus Mark ends the first major cycle of miracle stories and polemical dialogues (Mark 1:21–3:6) with the observation, "Then the Pharisees immediately went out and consulted with the Herodians as to how to destroy him" (3:6). We may probably take it that for Mark the chief reasons for this first manifestation of murderous intentions were that Jesus claimed authority to forgive sins ("blasphemy"); that he associated with tax-collectors and sinners; and that he healed on the sabbath.

In John too we find reflections intended to make intelligible to his readers the conflict between Jesus and his religious and social environment, and his ultimate execution. These reflections, however, are on a different level than in Mark and the other synoptic writers. This is essentially because of Johannine christology. For John Jesus is first and foremost the revealer of God in the world and the eschatological savior by whose agency and in relation to whom the salvation of the world and people is decided. In this context the divine sonship of Jesus and his messiahship also become central issues in the entire polemic. John portrays the dispute between Jesus and the Jews as a dispute about God and his revelation, which is in fact identical with Jesus the revealer. According to John the dispute is an out and out religious one, or, more accurately, it is a dispute about where the true revelation of God is to be found: in the Jewish religion or with Jesus and his followers. Consequently the question of true worship, the correct honoring of God, plays a central role in the gospel of John (cf. 2:12-22; 4:19-26). Consequently, too, the most important revelatory discourses, the ones that give rise to the conflict, are uttered in the synagogue (chap. 6; cf. 6:59) or in the temple at Jerusalem (chaps. 7, 8, 10).

If we compare this understanding of the matter with the synoptic accounts, we see immediately that the two conceptions are not easily harmonized. From a historical standpoint, the Johannine view is undoubtedly less probable than the synoptic. In dealing with John we must take into account that in large measure he is projecting the later view proper to his own tradition and community back into the time of Jesus. Above all, as regards the discussion with the Jews Ferdinand Hahn is right in saying:

16

In particular there is no mistaking the fact that what the evangelist has in view is not the situation in the first half of the first century A.D. but the situation created by the orthodox reorganization of Judaism after the catastrophe of the Jewish War. As a result, the period of John himself and the confrontation that has meanwhile arisen between Judaism and Christianity are to a large extent incorporated into the presentation. John is portraying a Judaism that has adopted a decidedly negative attitude to the Christian message.[27]

When we meet the expression "the Jews" in John, we must therefore distinguish two ideas:

a) the opposition between Jesus and the Jews. At this level there is question of God's revelation in Jesus and the religious self-understanding of the Jews. The latter, according to John, is determined by two things: the law and the temple cultus. Included here is the problem of Jesus' relationship to the Old Testament. In John the Old Testament is a subject of dispute, since both Jesus (as the Christ) and the Jews claim it as God's revelation.

b) the situation of John and his community, from within which they look back at the events of past history, across the intervening years and amid new circumstances. The definitive separation of the Church from Judaism has occurred; a polemical attitude, probably on both sides, is exerting its influence. As a result, the Jews become for John representatives of unbelief and of the unbelieving world that rejects Jesus. At this level, the execution of Jesus on the cross is the consequence of the unbelief of the world, a world that closes itself to the revealer and his message. It is of this that the prologue has already said, "And the light shines in the darkness, and the darkness did not comprehend it. . . . He was in the world, and the world was made by him, and yet the world did not recognize him. He came to what was his own, but his own did not receive him" (1:5, 10-11).

The critical dispute with Jesus, the proceedings between revealer and world, is a motif that runs through the entire gospel. It represents one of the basic structures of the fourth gospel, so that the passion narrative follows the inner logic of the Johannine presentation. The entire discussion regarding Jesus is presented in John in the form of a case "that is being tried between the Christian faith

17

and the world which is represented by the Jews"[28] and that reaches its final climax in the trial before Pilate. John the Baptist already refers to the outcome for Jesus when he says, "Behold the Lamb of God who takes away the sin of the world" (1:29). It can be said that in the first four chapters of the gospel the opposing sides are being distinguished and the parties slowly taking shape.

If we suppose with Bultmann[29] and Schnackenburg[30] that the correct sequence is chapter 6, then chapter 5, then according to chapter 6 a first great debate takes place in Galilee. In this debate the problem of political messianism plays a not unimportant role. The effect of the miracle of the loaves (6:1-15) is that the people are led by it to say, "This man is truly the prophet who is to come into the world." The text then continues, "When Jesus then realized that they would come and seize him *to make him king,* he withdrew once again to the mountain by himself " (6:15).

The entire discourse on the bread of life is also a debate between the revelation Jesus brings and Jewish messianic eschatology. The result is a first great division (6:60-71) at the end of which comes the first reference to Judas' act of betrayal. Then, in chapter 5, in connection with the healing of the paralytic at the Pool of Bethzatha (5:1-18), which John also presents as a conflict regarding the sabbath, the intention of putting Jesus to death is articulated for the first time: "For this reason the Jews sought all the more to kill him, because he not only abolished the sabbath but also called God his Father and thus made himself equal to God" (5:18).

In the story of the healing of the man born blind (chap. 9) the healing on the sabbath motif again plays a role (9:14, 16). There is a link here with the synoptic tradition. The healing on the sabbath motif appears again in the discussion of Jesus with the Jews in chapter 7 (vv. 22-23). But it is typical of John that the conflict reaches its full intensity only because of Jesus' claim to be revealer: "because he . . . called God his Father and thus made himself equal to God" (5:18c). In 7:19-20, 25, the Jews' intention of having Jesus killed is articulated once more, and again in connection with the miracle of healing in chapter 5.

The fact that the claim of Jesus to be revealer plays the decisive role in all this is made clear in the long dramatic discourse of 8:12-59, which reaches its climax in the revelatory statement, "Amen, amen, I tell you, before Abraham was, I am" (8:58). Here the Johannine Jesus describes himself as in fact the absolute eschatological revealer of God and claims for himself the unqualified divine "I am" of Exodus 3:14. This is undoubtedly the strongest formulation of a divine authority or divine claim on behalf of Jesus. The reaction of the Jews to this blasphemy is perfectly logical: "Then they picked up stones to throw at him. But Jesus hid himself and left the temple" (8:59).

There is a similar sequence connected with the discourse of Jesus on the feast of the Dedication (10:22-39). When Jesus says, "I and the Father are one," the listeners again want to stone him (10:30-31). When he asks why they wish to stone him and which of his works is the reason, he receives the answer, "It is not for a good work that we stone you, but for blasphemy, because you, a man, make yourself God" (10:32-33). The statement that Jesus, who is a man, makes himself God, may be said with some certainty to derive from the Jewish-Christian debate in which John is taking a position. But it also shows clearly that in John's eyes Jesus' claim to be revealer is what ultimately leads to his death, and this view of the background is to some extent correct in the eyes of the Christian community, where, of course, the acknowledgment and acceptance of Jesus is presupposed. At the same time, however, the Jewish view is not being simply distorted. For from the Jewish standpoint the idea of the divinity of Jesus is difficult to grasp even today.

The event that is decisive according to John's account and leads to the decree of death by the highest religious authorities in Judaism is the restoration of Lazarus to life (chap. 11). The incident is therefore narrated in great dramatic detail. The narrative is wholly geared to the proximate death of Jesus; the death and resuscitation of Lazarus are a symbolic anticipation of the death and victory of Jesus. In the dialogue of the disciples (11:7-10) the passion casts its shadow before it, as it does in Thomas's words, "Let us also go with him and die with him" (11:16). The historicity of the resuscitation of Lazarus causes scholars great difficulties.[31]

Whatever be the source from which he took the story, the evangelist with full deliberation places this greatest sign of Jesus the life-giver at this particular point in his gospel. In the dramatically intensifying struggle between faith and unbelief it acts as a final powerful impulse to faith, so that once again many people reach faith in Jesus (11:45), and the

19

Jewish leaders are greatly concerned by the swelling stream (11:48; 12:19). This forces them to mount a counterattack and officially to decree in the supreme council that Jesus must die. In the eyes of the evangelist, whose gaze penetrates beyond appearances, it is no accident that at the moment when the Son of God has revealed his power over life in an incomparable way, unbelieving men should decide to destroy him and should take all necessary steps to do so.[32]

As a matter of fact, it is highly revealing of John's way of looking at things that despite the heavily overstated presentation of the resuscitation of Lazarus he has a realistic eye for what is historically possible. Jesus did win followers and give rise to a mass movement, although probably not to the extent that the pious mind often imagines. At least there was the formation of a group large enough to catch the attention of the public. And this, for John, was the decisive reason why the supreme council proceeded against Jesus.

> Now many of the Jews who came to Mary and saw what he had done believed in him; some of them went to the Pharisees and told them what Jesus had done. Therefore the chief priests and Pharisees called a session of the supreme council and said: "What are we to do, since this man is performing so many miraculous signs? If we let him go on in this manner, everyone will believe in him, and the Romans will come and do away with our place and our people." One of them, Caiaphas, who was high priest of that year, said to them: "You are ignorant and do not understand that it is better for one man to die for the people than for the whole people to be destroyed." He said this, however, not of his own accord; rather, as high priest of that year, he prophesied that Jesus would die for the people, and not only for the people but in order that he might gather into unity the children of God scattered throughout the world. From that day forward they were determined to put him to death (11:45-53).

This text gives an account of the decision of the Sanhedrin to put Jesus to death and is a parallel to Mark 14:1-2 (10-11) par. It is thought, and correctly in all likelihood, that it belongs to the pre-

Johannine complex of traditions about the passion story and may well have formed the first part of the latter.[33] But even here John has substantially adapted and transformed the tradition. First of all, he describes the decision regarding Jesus' death as being the immediate consequence of the resuscitation of Lazarus. As John presents the situation, the miracles of Jesus have given rise to an immense mass movement, and there is danger that the great majority of the Jews are on the point of becoming followers of Jesus. Measured by the historical probabilities, this is in all likelihood much exaggerated, for it is only in their presentation by the fourth evangelist that the miracles of Jesus acquire their probative apologetic significance as signs.

In addition, it is primarily the Pharisees who come forward here as the important adversaries of Jesus.[34] This too is to be attributed to the way the fourth evangelist looks at the situation and again projects the circumstances of his own day back into the time of Jesus. At the time Jesus lived the Pharisees were indeed represented on the supreme council, but the Sadducees and the aristocracy of chief priests had a clear majority. Therefore, as we said earlier, the initiative in the proceedings against Jesus must have been controlled by the Sadducees, not the Pharisees. According to Mark 14:1-2 it is the chief priests and scribes who consider how Jesus is to be arrested and killed; in this Mark is more in accord with the historical facts.

At the same time, however, this passage of the fourth gospel is impressive for its realism in regard to the political situation. According to John the fact that the Jesus movement is threatening to become a mass movement causes the Sanhedrin with the high priest at its head to gather and even to admit their perplexity: "What are we to do?" To the enemies of Jesus the movement he headed was evidently a messianic political movement that could become dangerous. That is precisely the line of argument offered: If this continues, the Romans will intervene and destroy the (holy) place or temple and the people. Here again John is judging by later events. He is looking back to the destruction of the temple and the city of Jerusalem in A.D. 70. For him, then, the very thing the enemies of Jesus sought to prevent is what eventually happened. As he sees it, therefore, the enemy's political argument, which is not without a certain plausibility, contains a basic error with regard to Jesus. The political misunderstanding of the person and message of Jesus was to be paid for dearly. On this point Schnackenburg observes:

> On the surface this sounds like a political motive and as such should be attributed to the Sadducees who were the political realists. For their part, the Pharisees were prepared on other grounds to put up with the Roman yoke. When the evangelist presents things as he does, does he have better information or a better tradition than the synoptic writers (cf. Mark 14:1-2 par.) about the secret meeting of the supreme council? But perhaps he is simply reconstructing the thinking of the dominant circles of that earlier time in a way that approximates the historical truth.[35]

Even in this case the good historical judgment of John also depends on theology—not a moralizing theology, of course, but rather a theology of history. He is saying that unbelief caused the leaders of the people to be grotesquely blind when it came to the true welfare of their own nation; they made a tragic mistake. But, granted this fundamental bias, the enemies of Jesus argue quite logically, for it is the way of the world to drop an individual when he becomes a political danger to the cause.

> A wise prince, then, is not troubled about a reproach for cruelty by which he keeps his subjects united and loyal because, giving a very few examples of cruelty, he is more merciful than those who, through too much mercy, let evils continue, from which result murders or plunder, because the latter commonly harm a whole group, but those executions that come from the prince harm individuals only.[36]

Such is the political rule Caiaphas evidently intends to follow. The expression "Caiaphas, who was high priest of that year" certainly does not mean that John is proceeding on the assumption that the Jewish high priest's term of office was only for a year; this would represent stupendous ignorance. Caiaphas in fact held the office for a long time (A.D. 18-37, or nineteen years). The words "that year" probably refer to the year of Jesus' death and perhaps point to it as the "year of salvation."[37]

Caiaphas' advice that it is better for one man to die for the nation than for the entire nation to be destroyed may actually have been preserved in this form by the tradition. John, however, indicates a deeper meaning in it when he interprets "for the people" in a Christian sense. He justifies this interpretation by saying that the high priest probably had the gift of prophecy due to his office: "Along with seers and prophets there is found in the Hell[enistic]-Rom[an] period the prophetically gifted ruler who as priest-prince also has the charisma of prophecy."[38] According to Josephus, Hyrcanus I (135-104 B.C.) was particularly "thought worthy by God of possessing the three highest offices: the rulership of the people, the honor of the high priesthood, and the gift of prophesy."[39] But Caiaphas exercises his prophetic office unwittingly. He does not know that through his advice he is acting to serve the divine goal of salvation and that he is promoting the "salvation of the entire world" and not just of the Jewish nation.

In this statement John has probably given expression to what in his view was the most important cause of the passion to Jesus. To the eyes of faith the revelation of the divine love that seeks the salvation of the world reaches its climax in the death and resurrection of Jesus. In other words, God's plan of salvation is carried to its completion by the death of Jesus. But this takes place amid a web of very human intentions and plans, of political considerations and objectives in which error, cunning, and indifference play an important part, although when seen in the light of God's plan, all this, however farsighted it seems, once again proves to be in fact very shortsighted. Jesus is to be sacrificed in order to save the people from the Romans, and yet this very sacrifice will not hinder the destructive catastrophe but will rather hasten its coming.

THE STORY OF THE PASSION
(18:1–19:42)

Walk to the Mount of Olives;
Arrest of Jesus (18:1–11)[40]

John begins his account of the passion with a brief introduction. After finishing the farewell discourses Jesus goes out with his disciples to the other side of the brook Kidron, the side away from the city. There was a garden or grove there, and Jesus enters it with his disciples. The reason given for this is that Judas the traitor also knew the spot, "because Jesus often met there with his disciples" (vv. 1-2).

While Mark has Jesus speak his words about the conduct of the disciples and the denial of Peter as they are on their way to Mount Olivet, John has no need to do this, since Jesus has already spoken of all this in the farewell discourses (cf. 16:32; 13:36-38). The indication of place given in Mark is "to the Mount of Olives," where "there was a piece of land called Gethsemane" (Mark 14:26-32). John says only that "across the brook Kidron . . . there was a garden." There is no reason to doubt that both descriptions refer to the same place, namely the Mount of Olives which lay east of the city and was divided from it by the Kidron valley.

The precise notation "brook Kidron" is an example of John's concern, which can be seen elsewhere in the gospel as well, to locate various events as accurately as possible; we must allow that the evangelist had a good knowledge of local geography. The knowledge and concern are especially surprising since they stand in such strong contrast to the theological procedure and purpose of the gospel.[41] The important point John is making here is that Judas was familiar with the place since Jesus had often stayed there with his disciples.

This is an explanatory note of the evangelist who wishes to make it clear how the well-known events fit together.

To this place, then, Judas comes with a band of men to arrest Jesus (v.3). The detachment making the arrest is composed of a cohort (*speira*) as well as of servants "of the chief priests and Pharisees." This description evokes a strange picture, inasmuch as a cohort was a division of the Roman army and specifically one tenth of a legion: "Of the cohorts ten were 1,000 infantry strong; the other thirteen 600 infantry and 120 cavalry."[42] John evidently wants to convey the impression that the detachment making the arrest was fairly large, but also to make it clear from the beginning that the Romans and the Jewish leaders were collaborating. John may also want to heighten the contrast between the enemies of Jesus who in a worldly sense are numerous and powerful, and the defenseless, unarmed Jesus, especially since in a moment the relation of strength and weakness will be reversed.

According to Mark 14:43 the group that comes is simply a crowd (*ochlos*), sent by "the chief priests, scribes, and elders," and armed "with swords and clubs." In Mark's account, then, only the Jewish temple authorities were active in arresting Jesus. If we accept the idea that the Sadducees and therefore the aristocracy of chief priests as well were the real enemies of Jesus and the main instigators of his arrest, then the detachment sent for the arrest must have consisted essentially of members of the temple police. The latter "were at the disposal of the Sanhedrin. . . . They made arrests under the orders of the Temple overseers, and executed punishments under the direction of their leader."[43] The detachment may have been strengthened by servants of the reigning high priest, but hardly by Roman soldiers, as John supposes.[44] The Romans enter the scene only later, although it is possible that the Sanhedrin alerted the Romans in advance to their intentions.

While Mark (14:32-42 par.) recounts the prayer and struggle of Jesus in the Garden of Gethsemane and Luke describes the mortal fear of Jesus that is so intense as to force a bloody sweat, John mentions nothing even faintly similar. John has in large measure omitted the traits that show the deeply moving human side of Jesus: the fact that he felt fear in the face of approaching death and that he had first to make his way into the will of his heavenly Father, to pray his way into it, as it were. Yet this tradition was not entirely

26

unknown to him; 12:27-28 reminds us of the prayer in Mark 14:35-36: " 'Now is my soul anxious. Yet what am I to say? "Father, save me from this hour"? But it is for this purpose that I have come to this hour: Father, glorify your name!' Then a voice came from heaven: 'I have glorified it and will glorify it again.' "

It is at this point that we can put our finger directly on the difference between John's interpretation of the passion and that of the synoptic writers. John knows the tradition that before his arrest Jesus asked God to let the cup of suffering pass him by and to rescue him from this "hour of suffering." But this tradition did not fit in with the Johannine picture of Jesus as the victor over the cosmic powers, the conqueror of death. No, Jesus did not want to be saved "from this hour," but was wholly concerned with the glorification of God and his own glorification by God, even in suffering! The very question, "Am I not to drink the cup the Father has given me?" (18:11) shows that John knows the synoptic tradition regarding Gethsemane but has reshaped it. As John tells it, the story of Jesus' passion is from its outset the story of his triumph.

This becomes clear in a passage (vv. 4-9) which is entirely invented and organized by the evangelist and has no basis in the history of the tradition. Despite the overwhelming numerical superiority of the arresting detachment, Jesus is not only unafraid but remains the one in control and who dominates the entire scene. The situation is like the one described in 7:32, 45-52, where the servants who were to seize Jesus were powerless against him and were forced to return to their superiors without having accomplished their mission, and who even showed themselves deeply impressed by what Jesus said. On the present occasion, unless Jesus had been willing to let himself be arrested because he knew and accepted that the hour determined by the Father was at hand, the police would have been powerless against him. Verse 4 emphasizes once again something that is clear from the farewell discourses: Jesus knows everything that will happen to him; he is not simply caught up passively in events but will decisively control the course of them.

Consequently, he steps forward and meets the detachment with a question, "Whom do you seek?" The answer comes, "Jesus of Nazareth." And Jesus in turn replies, "I am he." The Greek words are *Ego eimi* and recall the christological *I am* formulas which express the majesty of Jesus. Here, of course, the immediate point of the

27

words is simply to identify Jesus, a point emphasized by the distinction made in verse 8: "I told you: I am he [i.e. the Jesus of Nazareth whom you seek]; if you are looking for me, then let these others go."

Yet there can be no doubt that for John, with his preference for a plurality of meanings, Jesus' consciousness of his own majesty also echoes in the words of self-identification, "I am he." This is clear from the reaction of the police, at whose side Judas the traitor, the former disciple, now stands, as is expressly noted (v. 5b). At the words "I am he" they all retreat and fall to the ground.

At this point, of course, the text has a purely symbolic and not a historical meaning. The aim is to bring home to the reader or hearer of the text, in a sensible, graphic way, the complete impotence of Jesus' enemies and, in contrast, the divine superiority of Jesus. Jesus is completely beyond the world's reach. It has no power to seize and arrest him unless he himself is willing to be seized and grants permission as it were. The incident is not to be understood as something from a fairy tale nor, on the other hand, as a miracle. In John, too, after all, the death of Jesus really takes place. Nor is John distinguishing between the man Jesus and the divine Christ, as many gnostic doctrines did.

Irenaeus of Lyons reports, for example:

> A certain Cerinthus in Asia taught that the world was made not by the first God but by a certain power already separate and distinct from the Power above all, and ignorant of the God above all. He supposed that Jesus was born not of a virgin but of Joseph and Mary, like all other men, and he became more righteous, more prudent, and more wise than all. After his baptism, from the Absolute Sovereignty above all the Christ descended upon him in the form of a dove; then he proclaimed the unknown Father and worked miracles. *At the end, the Christ withdrew from Jesus; Jesus suffered and was raised, but the Christ remained impassible, since he was spiritual.*[45]

We do not find in John this kind of christological dualism with its radical and essential distinction of the man Jesus from the heavenly Christ. On the contrary, John speaks of Jesus Christ, the "divine Word made flesh."

The impregnability of Jesus, as John pictures it, is based, in the final analysis, on his union with his Father, with God. In his passion Jesus stands completely unprotected against the concentrated power of the world. Humanly speaking, he even succumbs to it. But because of his union with God, the oneness with God proper to him as Son of the Father, he remains superior to the power of the world even in the defeat of death. This is an example of the general truth that our relationship to God makes us impregnable to the unconditioned determination of other human beings to manipulate us. When we seek to make our relationship to God, our faith in God, a reality as Jesus did, the power or domination of others over us is destroyed. Under these conditions, death manifests the powerlessness of the mighty and the might of the powerless. This is the real point John is making in this symbolic scene.

Once Jesus has made clear to those who would seize him how powerless they really are against him, he asks them the question a second time in order to surrender himself to them (vv. 7-8). His second response—"I told you that I am he; if you are looking for me, then let these others go" (v.8)—makes clear once again the orderly way, free of all panic, in which the arrest of Jesus takes place according to John. We hear nothing of a flight of the disciples. Rather, Jesus himself sees to it that there is no confusion about who is to be arrested. He thus shows himself to be also the good shepherd who remains solicitous to the end for the life and safety of his flock.

In verse 9 the evangelist reflects that in thus acting Jesus fulfills something he had said in his final prayer: "I have not lost a single one of those you gave me" (17:12). John cites these words of Jesus as a Scripture that is fulfilled after the manner of a Scripture; this is an indication that in his mind there is no longer any objective distinction between the word of God and the word of Jesus.

John has taken over from the tradition the little episode of the "attempt at resistance by a disciple who cuts off an ear of one of the servants" (18:10-11).[46] Mark has this brief account, "But one of those who were standing near drew his sword, struck the high priest's servant, and cut off his ear" (14:47). That is all; the next words of Jesus in Mark make no reference to the incident. Neither the name of the assailant nor the name of the servant is given. From a historical point of view it is rather unclear whether any such outward resistance was in fact offered; if it was, it was minor. Moreover, we ask quite naturally why in this case the much stronger arresting party

29

did not immediately strike back and single out the resister from the other disciples or even arrest all the other disciples along with Jesus. The view that at the arrest of Jesus a brawl started and led to a violent conflict and that Mark 14:47 has preserved a small reflection of this, is extremely improbable, since all the accounts speak of proceedings against Jesus alone and not against his disciples or even any one of them. The brief statement in Mark is probably intended only to heighten the defenselessness and nonviolence of Jesus; in actual fact there was no real resistance at all.

It is all the more interesting, then, that the other three evangelists have developed Mark's brief report into an edifying story. Matthew makes it the occasion for a teaching on the renunciation of force. Jesus speaks these weighty words to the assailant, who continues to be nameless in Matthew's account, "Put your sword in its scabbard. For all who take the sword will perish by the sword. Or do you think that I could not ask my Father and he would not immediately send more than twelve legions of angels to help me? But then how would the Scripture be fulfilled that this is how it must be?" (Matt. 26:52-54). In Luke Jesus shows himself even in this dangerous situation to be the unwearied savior and helper of people: "But Jesus answered and said, 'Stop! No more!' And he touched the ear and healed it" (Luke 22:57).

John retells the episode in his own way. We learn the name of the assailant: it is no other than Simon Peter himself. The name of the man who was struck is Malchus, which is possibly a Syrian name ("Mr. King"). The naming of the two is part of a growing legend about persons. The fact that Peter resists and draws his sword is very characteristic of Peter as depicted in the Johannine tradition: he is a passionate person and would do this kind of thing. The servant is mentioned again in another context (18:26). It is entirely incredible, however, that if Peter had really drawn his sword, they would have let him escape scot-free.

The answer Jesus gives Peter is of interest: "Put your sword in its scabbard. Am I not to drink the cup the Father has given me?" (v. 11). It reminds us of the answer Jesus gives in Matthew or at least is along same lines: armed resistance is rejected; chosen instead is the fulfillment of God's will by the acceptance of suffering. Here again we have an echo of the Markan Gethsemane tradition. But even in this episode the superiority of Jesus continues to be an important consideration. The resistance episode only serves to make even more manifest the very way in which Jesus evaluates things.

The Interrogation before Annas; Peter's Denial (18:12–27)

In John's account Jesus' captors first bring him to Annas (vv. 12-14). This scene is followed by the first part of Peter's denial (vv. 15-18). Next comes the actual interrogation before Annas (vv. 19-24) and finally the second part of the denial.

John's accounts of the interrogation before Annas and the denial of Peter are interlocking; a similar interlocking is already to be seen in the Markan presentation (Mark 14:58). It is probable that Peter's denial was handed down in close connection with the arrest and interrogation of Jesus by the Jews (high priest and Sanhedrin) and was not a fully independent tradition. This is consistent with the local setting, since the denial of Peter took place in the courtyard, that is, the immediate neighborhood of the high priest's palace. There is no need to doubt this statement.

For the rest, John and Mark (along with the synoptics generally) diverge considerably. Mark's account (14:53-65, 67, 72) shows two clearly distinct wholes: (a) the interrogation of Jesus before the Sanhedrin; (b) the denial of Peter. Verse 54, "Peter meanwhile followed him at a distance, even into the courtyard of the high priest; and he sat down by the fire with the servants and was warming himself," establishes the connection between the two wholes.

As for the interrogation before the Sanhedrin, Mark relates that Jesus is brought in to the high priest, in whose house "all the chief priests, elders, and scribes" are gathered or, in a word, the entire Sanhedrin or supreme council (Mark 14:53). Then a regular interrogation begins (Mark 14:55-59). They look for testimony that will enable them to condemn Jesus to death, but they find none. Many "false witnesses" (Mark's description) come forward against Jesus, but no consistent testimony emerges. One bit of the testimony against Jesus is recorded by Mark: "We heard him say, 'I will destroy this temple built by hands and after three days I will build another

31

not made by hands' " (Mark 14:58). These are words that Jesus may actually have spoken on some occasion—John knows them too (2:19-21)—and that may indeed have come up in the interrogation.

According to Mark the questioning of the witnesses leads nowhere. The high priest therefore endeavors to force a decision. As president of the Sanhedrin he himself now takes over the questioning of Jesus, the accused (Mark 14:60-64), but at first receives no answer. Then he asks Jesus directly, "Are you the Messiah, the Son of the Blessed One?" To this Jesus answers, according to Mark, "I am! And you will see the Son of man sitting at the right hand of the Power and coming with the clouds of heaven." Matthew's version of this entire scene is the one most familiar to us (26:62-66) but in its solemnly dramatic form it is a development of the Markan text by Matthew the evangelist. The high priest then tears his garments as a sign of his indignation and says, "What further need have we of witnesses? You have heard the blasphemy. What is your judgment?" There is universal agreement in condeming Jesus to death.

Thus, in Mark's presentation, the Jews undertook an established type of judicial proceeding against Jesus; witnesses were heard and at the end the sentence of death was pronounced. At the same time, there is an easily recognizable tendency in Mark to represent the interrogation of the witnesses against Jesus as unsatisfactory and disappointing in its results, and to see as the decisive grounds for the death sentence Jesus' own claim to be the Messiah, "the Son of the Blessed One" or else his identification of himself with the "Son of man." Scholars have shown, however, that this presentation of the matter raises many unresolved problems.[47] The main problem is that the claim to be Messiah could not, in Jewish law, be stigmatized as blasphemous; it was not a crime subject to the punishment of death. We must therefore assume that we have before us a Christian and specifically a Markan version of this judicial hearing.

As far as historical fact is concerned, we may suppose that the supreme council did in fact examine Jesus, but not that there was a regular judicial proceeding with a death sentence at its end. One reason why there was in all likelihood no such proceeding is that in the period of Roman domination the Sanhedrin had no authority to impose the death penalty and carry it out. When Judea became a Roman province in A.D. 6 and thus was placed directly under the

32

emperor, Coponius was sent as first procurator "with authority from Caesar to inflict the death penalty."[48] It is clear, therefore, that the supreme council no longer possessed this power, since two competing jurisdictions with the power of inflicting capital punishment are hardly conceivable.

Consequently, if the Jews wanted Jesus executed, they had to approach the Roman procurator. In order to do so, they had to adduce plausible legal grounds that could convince the procurator. These grounds they found in the concept of political messiahship. They could with some reason suspect Jesus of activity that was politically dangerous; on the other hand, it was quite natural to think of political leaders as being messianic pretenders. The examination before the Sanhedrin, which met under the presidency of the high priest, had as its primary aim to provide the grounds required if the Roman procurator was to pass sentence. These grounds could be summed up under the catchword "messianic pretender."

The Sanhedrin possessed supreme religious and legal authority in Judaism; it had seventy members, plus one, the president, who was the high priest. In Jesus' day, the Sadducees had a strong majority on the council; previous high priests were also represented. It is probable that some Pharisaic scribes were also members.[49] Consequently, Mark's account of the trial of Jesus before the supreme council does contain a historical nucleus and cannot be described as unqualifiedly unhistorical. On the other hand, in its present form it shows, especially in the solemn messianic confession of Jesus, a number of traits that originated in the primitive Christian profession of faith in the messiahship of Jesus.

Peter's denial likewise enjoys the presumption of being historical fact; no one would have invented such a highly compromising action for the leading man in the primitive community. The "incident at Antioch" which Paul mentions (Gal. 2:11-17) shows that unwavering firmness was apparently not a virtue of the historical Peter. Then, too, the words, "Before the cock crows, you will deny me three times" (cf. Mark 14:34, 72; Matt. 26:34, 75; Luke 22:34, 61-62; John 13:38), may well be those of the historical Jesus; Jesus may have said them on such an occasion to Peter who seems often to have talked too big. The fact that the accounts of the denial speak of a triple denial by Peter probably means that the story was shaped in

33

accordance with the words of Jesus in the tradition, in order to show them being fulfilled with literal exactness. From a historical viewpoint, however, a single denial seems more likely.

If we compare John's account with Mark's, the following differences in emphasis immediately prove important. According to Mark, the crucial point in the trial of Jesus is his examination by the supreme Jewish judicial authority, the high priest and the Sanhedrin. The proceedings before Pilate are seen as simply the necessary consequence; in Mark the Roman procurator acts as the agent who carries out the wishes of the Jewish authorities when he finally gives in to pressure from the crowd. The fact that he had the final say is not sufficiently clear in Mark's account.

Not so in John. In this account of the passion the decisive trial is the one conducted by the Roman procurator; the proceedings before Pilate are the dramatic climax of the narrative. Apart from this, John mentions only an examination before the high priest Annas who is no longer in office. In 18:34 it is said that Jesus was sent to Caiaphas, but we do not learn what happened there. John says nothing of an examination or even a legal proceeding before the supreme council. Did he know nothing of any such proceedings? Or did he deliberately omit mention of them? We shall see in a moment that in his presentation John could not use the kind of climax we find in Mark. In Mark's portrayal the solemn messianic confession of Jesus, his self-revelation before the supreme tribunal, is in fact the christological culmination of the entire gospel. In John, on the other hand, this kind of ultimate statement about the sovereignty of Jesus occurs much earlier in the gospel (e.g., 8:58; 10:22-39), so that there is no room now for the kind of scene Mark uses.

There is thus no reason to doubt the accuracy of the way John depicts the first examination. This does not tell us, however, just what tradition John had before him; that is a question which we must in honesty leave open. It is impossible to harmonize the two accounts of John and Mark by saying, for example, that Jesus was taken to Annas' house where a first, preliminary examination took place, until all the members of the supreme council could be called together late at night; then the decisive Jewish proceedings took place before the Sanhedrin, after which Jesus was brought before Pilate, and we pick up the story again in John. This effort at har-

34

monization is an obfuscation that does not do justice to the various texts. We must allow each of the presentations to stand on its own. But then it is noteworthy that the Johannine account, which knows of only a single examination of Jesus by the Jews and in which the real judicial proceedings take place before the Roman procurator, the person with the ultimate authority, is also regarded by historical critics as the more likely account.

JESUS BEFORE ANNAS (18:12–14)

The arresting squad of Romans (the cohort and its commander) and Jews ("servants of the Jews") take Jesus prisoner and bring him first to Annas. We are then given a more detailed description of Annas. He is the father-in-law of Caiaphas, the "high priest of that year," that is, the year of Jesus' death. Caiaphas himself is identified by a reference back to 11:49-51: He is the one who had at that time advised the Jews that it was better that one man die for the nation. If John recalls that incident here, he evidently does so in order to tell us that he regards Caiaphas and his advice as chiefly responsible for the death of Jesus.

Annas or Ananus

held the office of high priest from A.D. 6 to A.D. 15. He was head of a priestly family that, upon his accession, began to supplant the family of Boëthus, which was related to the house of Herod and had hitherto dominated the priest-hood. . . . Quirinius probably chose him to be high priest because he was one of those Sadducees and men of substance who for years had been advocating a Roman regime, and also because he had played a leading role in the fall of Archelaus; it was a political appointment tendered to a man whom Quirinius trusted. Not only did Annas reorganize the High Council at Jerusalem and preside over it during his period in office, he also dominated it from the time he was removed from office in 15 until his death in 35.[50]

Josephus says of him, "This elder Ananus must have been one of the happiest of men, for he had five sons, all of whom served the Lord as high priest after he himself had occupied this position of honor for a long time."[51] This is enough to explain his influence; here, once again, the reliability of John's information is surprising.

PETER'S DENIAL (18:15–18)

Like the synoptic writers, John is familiar with the tradition that the leading disciple, Simon Peter, did not play a creditable role in the arrest and trial of Jesus but on the contrary denied his Lord and master. Yet we cannot really be entirely negative in our judgment of Peter, since out of curiosity or an initial courage he at least followed Jesus and the arresting squad as far as the courtyard of the high priest's mansion. According to Mark 14:54, 66, Peter was the only one to follow Jesus.

John, however, already suggests other motifs and possibilities, telling us that with Peter another disciple followed Jesus. This other disciple, he says, was known to the high priest; initially he follows Jesus into the courtyard of the high priest while Peter remains standing outside at the gate to the premises of the high priest. The passage reminds us of 20:3-10 and of 20:4 in particular, where in a similar way the other disciple goes with Simon Peter to see the empty tomb on Easter morning, and the other disciple again has a certain precedence over Peter.

Interpreters have been fond of seeing in this other disciple "the disciple whom Jesus loved" and whom tradition identified with the apostle John as author of the fourth gospel. All this has become quite doubtful today; it is practically impossible for us to identify this unnamed other disciple with any historical personage. We know only that he appears suddenly a number of times in the gospel and plays what to some extent is a key role. It is possible that the author of the gospel and his circle of friends saw in this other disciple a well known and important person. In the present context he serves only to explain how Peter is able to enter the courtyard: the other disciple is familiar with the place and is known to the high priest and his servants; consequently he can arrange to have the gatekeeper let Peter into the courtyard. Having done this he has accomplished his purpose and plays no further part.

At this point the servant girl who is acting as gatekeeper imme-diately asks Peter, "Are you too one of this man's disciples?" and

Peter utters his first denial, "I am not." He then joins the slaves and servants of the high priest who have lit a fire to warm themselves in the cold night. "Peter too stood with them and was warming himself" (cf. Mark 14:67). In comparison with Mark John has made the story more vivid.

THE INTERROGATION BEFORE ANNAS (18:19–24)

In this examination the high priest, Annas, asks Jesus "about his disciples and his teaching" (v. 19). The answer Jesus gives is both remarkable and typical of the Johannine approach to the story. In its context here the answer is first of all a refusal to give the high priest a clear answer. While in Mark 14:62 Jesus makes a clear confession of messiahship to the high priest and the supreme council, the Johannine Jesus strictly refuses such a confession. Instead he refers to his earlier public activity.

This answer is fully in accord with the Johannine theology of revelation. According to John Jesus is the revealer of God to the cosmos; his word and revelation are therefore directed to the world, and this includes the public world. This publicity is somewhat more clearly defined in terms of the public places in which Jesus has discoursed; he mentions the synagogue and the temple. Thus, for example, the discourse on the bread of life (6:22-58) took place in the synagogue at Capernaum (6:59). Jesus usually gave his other great discourses in the temple at Jerusalem.[52] There too he had made his weighty statements about his function as revealer of God and savior; there he had spoken, even if in an ambiguous, veiled, and mysterious manner, about his messiahship.

For the reader who has read through the gospel of John to this point, Jesus' answer affords no difficulties. In his revelatory discourses Jesus had likewise always issued the decisive demand that people believe in his word and in himself. He has really nothing more to say now. Any further statement would only be a repetition of what he had said earlier.

Perhaps the evangelist also intends to expose as hypocritical Annas' question about Jesus' "disciples and teaching." If the high priest has already had a part in the decision to kill Jesus and then in his arrest, he certainly knows by now the accusations laid against Jesus,

37

his disciples, and his teaching. If the Jews, who were accustomed to gather publicly in synagogue and temple, were acquainted with Jesus' teaching, then it may be assumed that the dominant circles in Judaism had not remained ignorant of it.

Finally, John contrasts the public discourses of Jesus with a "speaking in secret." Jesus preaches no esoteric secret doctrine (like many apocalyptic preachers, for example, or the Qumran sect, or other mystico-esoteric groups). This distinction between public and therefore generally known or at least accessible teaching, on the one hand, and a secret teaching, on the other, can also be regarded as an apologetic argument directed to those outside. To the public world of paganism the Christian faith does not represent a dangerous or obscene secret teaching, any more than it did formerly to the public world of the Jews; the Christian communities, though united by a faith, are not secret sects dangerous to the state.

For the evangelist public debate with the Jews is now at an end. The final debate in which life or death is the issue will take place before the judgment seat of Pilate, the Roman procurator.

The description of the interrogation that John gives us is instructive inasmuch as it shows that Annas, the member of the priestly aristocracy, and Jesus of Nazareth, the captured revealer, have nothing to say to one another. Notable here again is the inherent superiority of Jesus, a quality further emphasized in the immediately ensuing incident. As in Mark 14:65 Jesus is mistreated; one of the bailiffs of the court slaps Jesus on the cheek and says, "Is that how you answer the high priest?" (v. 22). This is the officiousness of a servile underling. But in fact Jesus is honoring Annas in a different way: by not surrendering either self-respect or respect for the truth in the face of this examining magistrate who really has no authority. Unlike Paul, for example (Acts 23:1-5), Jesus does not defend himself but, without being either provocative or letting himself be provoked, insists simply but firmly on his right, "If I have said anything wrong, show me that it is wrong; but if I have spoken the truth, why do you strike me?" (v. 23). In his *Passion according to John* J. S. Bach has interpreted the passage as expressing a sense of intense interior shock.

Then, says John, Annas sent Jesus bound to Caiaphas (v. 24); it is left entirely to the reader to guess what may have happened there. Since speculation on this point will not help the reader to a better understanding of the text, we shall not indulge in it. Nor is there any profit in trying to harmonize Mark and John, since the two represent different approaches.

PETER'S FURTHER DENIAL (18:25–27)

With a few strokes of his pen John completes the scene of Peter's denial. Here again he expands upon the tradition. Simon Peter is still standing among the slaves and servants and warming himself at the fire. Now these people ask him, "Are not you also one of his disciples?" Again Peter denies it. According to Mark 14:69-70 it is the maidservant who asks Peter this question a second time and she is followed by other bystanders; comparison shows how John has altered the tradition. This is even clearer in the third question. This time it is one of the high priest's servants, and specifically a "relation of the man whose ear Peter had cut off," who turns to him and says, "Didn't I see you with him in the garden?" As a matter of historical fact it is hard to imagine that the soldiers or police would have reacted so mildly to active resistance; but for John's presentation the resistance was important because it now makes possible a crescendo in the questioning of Peter (similarly in 21:15-17). John is not unacquainted with the techniques of dramatic effect. The effect is further intensified by the final statement, "Again Peter denied it, and immediately the cock crowed" (v. 27).

Here the story ends; we are told nothing of Peter's reaction. Not so in the synoptic telling of the tale; cf. Mark 14:72: "And he immediately began to weep" (cf. also Matt. 26:75), or especially Luke 22:61-62: "The Lord turned around and looked at Peter, and Peter remembered the words the Lord had spoken to him: 'Today before a cock crows, you will deny me three times.' And he went out and wept bitterly."

Jesus before Pilate (18:28–19:16)

The proceedings before Pilate form the natural dramatic climax of the Johannine passion narrative. It is here too that the final conflict of the Jews with Jesus takes place. Yet Jesus has nothing more to

39

say to the Jews; he remains mute toward them. There are only two conversations between Jesus and Pilate, but they are theologically significant. Let us recall, to begin with, the *synoptic accounts*. The presentation by Mark, whom Matthew and Luke follow, although they make numerous additions, is clear and lucidly organized.

The decision to hand over Jesus (Mark 15:1; cf. Matt. 27:1-2; Luke 23:1). Mark reports a further resolution taken by the Sanhedrin: "And as soon as morning came the chief priests, elders, and scribes, and the entire supreme council passed a resolution; they bound Jesus, led him away, and handed him over to Pilate." Matthew 27:1 explains that the resolution in question concerned putting Jesus to death. Pursuant to it, Jesus was handed over to Pilate.

According to Josephus, Jeshua son of Ananias, a prophet of doom, was likewise seized by prominent citizens of Jerusalem and beaten and abused. Although he offered no resistance, neither was he deterred from continuing to prophesy the downfall of Jerusalem. "The Jewish authorities, rightly concluding that some supernatural force was responsible for the man's behaviour, took him before the Roman procurator."[53] There he was scourged, but once it was realized that he represented no political danger, he was released. According to K.-H. Müller, in a passage we cited earlier, what we have here is "a set sequence of judicial proceedings: the Sadducean aristocracy lay violent hands on the prophet of doom, interrogate him while beating him, and finally hand him over to the procurator who has the offender scourged and likewise subjects him to an official inquiry."[54] There is no significant objection to assuming that this sequence of judicial proceeding was already the usual practice in the time of Jesus. For we must postulate that the various legal and political competences of the Sanhedrin and the Roman procurator were established from the very beginning (A.D. 6) of the period when procurators ruled in Palestine, especially since the Sadducees, led by Annas, expressly supported and welcomed the establishment of procuratorial government in place of the ethnarchy of Archelaus, son of Herod the Great.

The examination before Pilate (Mark 15:2-5; Matt. 27:11-14; Luke 23:2-3). Mark's account is extremely brief. Pilate asks Jesus, "Are you the king of the Jews?" This doubtless represents the decisive accusation; "king of the Jews" was the label put on messianic claim-

40

ants of power, and the messianism in question was thoroughly political. Consequently, the accusation was meant to be a political one. Jesus answers, "You say so." The answer can be taken in two ways: "Yes, it is so," or "*You* say it, not I." In any case, we cannot judge from Mark's account what Jesus may in fact have said, since in Mark the Christian understanding of messiahship is also conveyed in the words and is even, in all probability, their primary content. One thing is certain: Jesus made no claim to be a political Messiah; he had no desire to be "king of the Jews" in a political sense. This understanding of the phrase is therefore excluded in Mark's mind.

This means there are only two possibilities left. Either Jesus gives another meaning to the concept "king of the Jews" (as is the case in John) or he wants to say that Pilate might give the idea a political interpretation but that he himself clearly rejects any such interpretation. (Therefore: "You say so; the assertion is yours, not mine.") My own conjecture is that Jesus did not endorse this political conception at all, because he could in no way identify with it, and that Mark subsequently gave Jesus' answer (as he, Mark, formulated it) a Christian meaning, turning it into a confession of Jesus as Messiah.

According to Mark, the examination consisted only of this one question of the procurator and this one answer of Jesus. The text then continues, "And the chief priests made many accusations against him" (v. 3). Pilate then questioned the accused again but received no further answer, "so that Pilate was very surprised."

Matthew 27:11-14 follows Mark except for unimportant changes. Luke (23:2-3), however, rewords the Markan tradition to his own liking. In my judgment the changes and additions in Luke's narrative are not to be attributed to supplementary sources or traditions, but must be attributed entirely to the redactor of this gospel.[55] For Luke evidently felt the lack in Mark of a formal charge against Jesus, and decided that he must supply one. In his account it reads, "We have found that this man is alienating our nation; he bars the payment of taxes to the emperor, and claims to be the Messiah, the King" (Luke 23:2). Thereupon, as in Mark, Pilate begins the interrogation with the question, "Are you the King of the Jews?'" After this question, which is by no means unimportant and certainly not without its dangers, Pilate does not go into the matter of refusing the imperial tax, as he probably would have if there had really been any question of it. It would then have been no problem for the procurator to condemn Jesus for Zelotic machinations. This item in the charge originated therefore with Luke.

In 23:4-12 Luke introduces a lengthy passage motivated chiefly by the desire to see the political authorities expressly affirm the innocence of Jesus. Immediately after this first examination Pilate says, "I find no guilt in this man" (v. 4). At this the chief priests and the crowd urge the charge against Jesus by saying, "He stirs up the people with his teaching throughout Judea, from Galilee even to here" (v. 5). When Pilate hears that Jesus is from Galilee, he sends him to his own political superior, Herod Agrippa, for sentencing. According to Luke, this leads to an awkward situation, since Herod expects Jesus to perform all sorts of striking signs and wonders, but is disappointed in his expectation. "Herod and his entourage treated him with contempt and mocked him. They clothed him in a white robe and sent him back to Pilate. On that day Herod and Pilate became friends; previously they had been enemies to one another" (Luke 23:6-12).

There has been a good deal of puzzled speculation as to the precise point of this scene.[56] J. Blinzler's view is that the episode of Herod is historical. It "is reported only by Luke, but the slightness of documentation does not justify our doubting the historicity of the incident. The matter peculiar to the Third Evangelist includes a whole series of incidents of absolutely unimpeachable historicity."[57] And again:

> Luke 23:9 makes it clear enough why the Tetrarch had wanted to see Jesus. He was hoping for a showy miracle. Only if we do violence to the text can the mocking of Jesus be construed as a condemnation. . . . The most obvious interpretation of his sending the accused back to Pilate is doubtless that the Tetrarch was not prepared to take the case off the procurator's hands.[58]

This explanation in no way makes the whole business more plausible. The only thing clear is that Luke is undoubtedly more interested in Herod Agrippa that are the other evangelists.[59] Especially to be noted is Luke 9:7-9, and verse 9 in particular: "Herod said: 'I had John beheaded. Who then is this man of whom I hear such things?' And he sought thereafter to see him." This wish of Herod is finally granted: "When Herod saw Jesus, he was very glad; for he had long wanted to see him" (23:8). Thus it is Luke himself who establishes the link between the two passages.

The decisive reason for the story is undoubtedly that Luke means both authorities, Pilate and Herod, to acknowledge the innocence of Jesus, and this is precisely what happens: "You have brought this man to me as one who stirs up the people. See, I have questioned him in your presence and have found the man to be not guilty in regard to the matters of which you have accused him. Herod too found him not guilty, for he has sent him back to us. Evidently, he has done nothing deserving of death" (23:14-15). In Acts 4:26-28 Luke again mentions the collaboration of Herod and Pilate, this time as an interpretation of Ps. 2:1-2 and especially of the verse, "The kings of the earth rise up and the princes conspire against the Lord and his anointed." Luke thus makes it clear that his aim in this episode is to have the political authorities acknowledge the innocence and political harmlessness of Jesus; if two such important witnesses say it, it must be so. The second reason for the incident is that the Scripture may be fulfilled. The episode does not represent a historical event.

Jesus and Barabbas (Mark 15:6-15; Matt. 27:15-26; Luke 23:18-25). Mark and, following him, the other synoptic evangelists now tell of an attempt by Pilate to rescue Jesus from the condemnation and execution that threaten him, by means of a kind of plebescite in connection with an act of amnesty. Mark's story is that for the feast day—he evidently means the feast of Passover, the greatest feast of the Jews—Pilate freed a prisoner, anyone they requested. Matthew (27:15) interprets Mark's remark as referring to a regular, fixed custom: the procurator was accustomed to release a prisoner to the people. This remark is the point of reference for the much discussed question of a *privilegium paschale*, a Passover amnesty, as a fixed custom. Mark/Matthew presuppose such a custom and use it as the basis for the Barabbas incident.

The prisoner whose freedom is the issue in this situation is named *Barabbas*. According to a reading in the Caesarean text of Matthew his name was *Jesus Barabbas;* a good many scholars regard this reading as the true one.[60] Mark says of Barabbas that he had been arrested along with a group of insurgents who had committed a murder in the course of an uprising; possibly Barabbas was regarded as the leader of the insurgents. The crowd comes to Pilate's official

43

residence, impelled by the wish to ask for the prisoner's release. At this point, according to Mark, Pilate intervenes with a question, "Do you want me to release the king of the Jews to you?" Pilate realized that the chief priests had been motivated by envy, that is, in more general terms, by an evil intention, in handing Jesus over to him. The chief priests immediately see what Pilate is after, and they now incite the crowd to ask the procurator for the release of Barabbas instead; the crowd does so. Thereupon Pilate asks a second question, "What shall I do with the man you call the king of the Jews?" The answer is short and terse, "Crucify him!" Pilate counters, "What crime has he committed?" The same response comes back even more violently, "Crucify him!" At this, Pilate releases Barabbas in order to placate the mob. Jesus is first handed over to be scourged, after which he is to be crucified. Thus far Mark's account.

Matthew follows Mark for the most part but he introduces two important scenes. According to Matt. 27:19 Pilate's wife sends him a message while he is still presiding on the bench: Pilate is not to lay hands on "this just man. . . . for I have suffered much in a dream today because of him." The scene is meant primarily to emphasize the innocence of Jesus; he is a just, that is, a holy man, and it is a serious matter to do violence to such a one. There is an aura of the numinous about him. This scene is in all probability not historical.

The second scene is in Matt. 27:24-25: "When Pilate finally saw that he was getting nowhere and that the uproar was only increasing, he took water, washed his hands in the presence of the crowd, and said: 'I am innocent of the blood of this just man. You are responsible!' Then all the people replied saying: 'His blood be upon us and our children!' " The scene is well known because of its fateful symbolism. The washing of hands as a sign that there is no blood on them, that is, as a ritual of purification, needs no further explanation; Pilate washes his hands in innocence. By this public gesture he endeavors to throw off responsibility for Jesus. On the other hand, in order to get rid of Jesus, all the people, as Matthew explicitly notes (and he means in fact the entire Jewish people), declare themselves ready to take responsibility for his death with all its consequences present and future. That is what is meant by the words, "His blood be upon us and our children!"

This scene likewise has no historical basis. It is reported only by Matthew and is part of the material special to him. It is probably a sheer invention of the evangelist and intended to substantiate his view that the Jews were the ones chiefly responsible for the death of Jesus. We should not fail to note that Matthew is here using the category of Jewish collective guilt and that, even though there were indeed some Old Testament examples of such a category, he is laying on Christianity and the Church a heavy burden and even one that has proved disastrous in the course of the centuries. For only too often Christian anti-Semitism has appealed to these words for justification.

Luke (23:18-25) has made fewer changes in the text of Mark. He gives no reason why Barabbas is suddenly brought into the picture.[61] In addition, he dramatizes the incident: the crowd shouts, "Away with this man! Release Barabbas to us!" Barabbas is a lone wolf in Luke, and not the representative or head of a larger group of insurgents. Pilate's efforts to free Jesus are even greater in Luke; so too the procurator lays a stronger emphasis on Jesus' innocence: "What crime has he committed? I have found no basis in him for a sentence of death; I will have him scourged and then let him go." At the end Luke underscores the injustice and cruelty of the outcome: "He set free the man they asked for, the one who had been imprisoned for rebellion and murder; Jesus, however, he handed over to their will."

From a historical viewpoint the Barabbas incident raises a number of questions on which scholars are constantly renewing discussion. First of all, there is the question of a *regularly recurring Passover amnesty*. Thus far no evidence has been found for the existence of such an amnesty during the period when procurators governed Judea. There is some validity to the argument that if Josephus had known of such a privilege in favor of the Jews he would surely not have passed it over in silence. Other Jewish sources too are silent on the subject.

Blinzler,[62] indeed, has found a passage in the Mishnah[63] which reckons with someone being released from prison at Passover. From this Blinzler concludes, "The Mishna . . . permits the assumption that the release of an Israelite prisoner shortly before the evening of the paschal supper, i.e. on 14 Nisan, was at least a frequent, but most probably a regular occurrence. Hence, this Mishna text actually represents a notable support for the New Testament account of the Easter amnesty."[64]

It is correct that the scholars of the Mishnah discussed the possibility of a prisoner being released for the feast of Passover; nor
can it be doubted that in principle such a release was possible and
may well have occurred from time to time. But it is too big a step
to conclude from this occasional possibility to a usual practice, especially in the form of a regular amnesty. It is probable that Mark
was the first to deduce a custom of a Passover amnesty from some
particular instance. This brings us to the main point: even if such
a custom did not exist, the Barabbas incident as such may well be
historical, as many exegetes assume with good reason. Thus M.
Dibelius says, "Even though we know nothing of any such amnesty
as a custom, there is no reason to doubt the scene; the assumption
of invention would mean ascribing to the earliest reporters a plastic
propensity and a poetic power such as is not to be observed elsewhere in the narrative."[65]

The important thing is the meaning of the text: "Opposed to the
King of the Kingdom of God must be set a rival, one who is most
deeply involved in the world's iniquity."[66] It is highly likely that the
individual in question was the leader of a Zealot resistance group
and that the tradition is concerned primarily with the resultant
contrast: Jesus is indicted and crucified as "King of the Jews" because
he supposedly claimed messianic power, while the representative
of the party that really did represent politico-messianic ideas and
claims is let go free.

The fact that the proceedings against Jesus and the Barabbas
incident coincided was thus the result of chance. If the name Jesus
Barabbas is correct, there may in fact have been a confusion of the
two persons. It would not be something extraordinary for Pilate to
give in to pressure from the crowd. Of course, the belief that even
in such chance occurrences God's plan and action were in fact at
work was taken for granted by the early Christian witnesses, so that
even in this event they would see a deeper meaning.

*The mocking of Jesus as "king of the Jews" (Mark 15:6-20; Matt.
27:21-31).* According to Mark 15:15 (Matt. 27:20) Pilate had Jesus
scourged. No further details are given of this cruel punishment, in
which the customary instrument was whips with pieces of bone or
lumps of lead attached to the thongs. Many a criminal died while
being thus scourged. According to John, Pilate decreed this punishment in order to stir the Jews to pity. According to Mark and

Matthew it immediately preceded the crucifixion. In both versions it was evidently connected with the accompanying mocking. It was not unusual for soldiers to mock the poor creatures delivered into their hands, and a mocking of Jesus such as is described here is a historical possibility. In addition, the tradition shows that the primitive Church was quite aware of the problematic aspect of the accusation against Jesus of being "king of the Jews." Thus the treatment of Jesus as "king of fools" is not without its ambiguity.

The entire body of soldiers gathers, and all take part in the cruel game. They put a red cloak on Jesus, probably a soldier's cloak; it has to be red, because red is the color of the royal purple. A fool's crown or wreath is quickly woven and placed on his head, while a stick serves as a scepter. Once he has been dressed as king of fools, the homage begins. The soldiers approach him, do him homage in the form of a genuflection (*proskynēsis*), and say, "Hail, King of the Jews!" a greeting that echoes the *Ave, Caesar!* ("Hail, Caesar!"). Mistreatment accompanies this procedure. Since the soldiers were Romans, their contempt for the Jews probably found a vent here.

That such scenes of mocking were not unusual can be seen from a description given by Philo of Alexandria in his book *Against Flaccus*. When the Jewish king, Agrippa I, visited Alexandria in A.D. 38, he was mocked by the rabble of the city. They took a lunatic named Carabas, brought him to the Gymnasium, and

> set him up on high to be seen of all and put on his head a sheet of byblus spread out wide for a diadem, clothed the rest of his body with a rug for a royal robe, while someone who had noticed a piece of the native papyrus thrown away in the road gave it to him for his sceptre. And when as in some theatrical farce he had received the insignia of kingship and had been tricked out as a king, young men carrying rods on their shoulders as spearmen stood on either side of him in imitation of a bodyguard. Then others approached him, some pretending to salute him, others to sue for justice, others to consult him on state affairs. Then from the multitudes standing round him there rang out a tremendous shout hailing him as Marin, which is said to be the name for "lord" in Syria. For they knew that Agrippa was both a Syrian by birth and had a great piece of Syria over which he was king.[67]

47

This example gives us an idea of what a parodying of a king would be like; the parallelism with the mocking of Jesus (Mark 15:16-20) is clear. The likeness is hardly to be accounted for by literary dependence, but is due to the fact that in both cases a fixed royal ritual that was widespread throughout the Near East was being parodied or burlesqued. Investiture with the insignia of royalty, homage, and acclamation were all part of this ritual, and it did not take much imagination to parody it in the case of the king of fools.

Pontius Pilate.[68] Who was this man to whom it fell, as procurator of Judea, a high-level servant of the Roman state, to handle the case of Jesus of Nazareth and who as such became part of the Christian profession of faith: "suffered under Pontius Pilate"?

Pilate belonged to the Pontiani, a Roman family of the equestrian order, and was sent to Judea as procurator in the twelfth year of the reign of Tiberius; he was the fifth in the series of procurators of Judea and held the office for ten years (A.D. 26-36). A testimony cited by Philo describes him as "naturally inflexible, a blend of self-will and relentlessness" and mentions "the briberies, the insults, the robberies, the outrages and wanton injuries, the executions without trial constantly repeated, the ceaseless and supremely grievous cruelty."[69]

Pilate had many a time provoked the Jews by deliberately reckless actions. He did so right at the beginning of his governorship by having his soldiers enter Jerusalem at night with images of the emperor on their standards. This caused an immense uproar, since it was regarded as a major violation of the prohibition against images. It even led to a mass demonstration of Jews at Caesarea, the habitual official residence of the procurator; the demonstration did not cease until Pilate ordered the standards withdrawn from the city.[70]

On another occasion he angered the Jews by taking gold from the temple treasury, the Corban—which was regarded as sacred—in order to build a new aqueduct for Jerusalem. When a demonstration began, he had his soldiers disperse the crowd with whips; in the ensuing widespread panic many people died.[71] The repeated provocations, usually accompanied by the use of unjustifiable force, finally led to his removal from office in A.D. 36, by Vitellius, governor of Syria. Vitellius ordered Pilate to Rome to render an account to the emperor, but before he reached Rome Tiberius had died.[72] We have no certain knowledge of Pilate thereafter. "The *Christian legend* makes Pilate either end his own life by suicide, or suffer death at the hands of the emperor as punishment for his proceedings against Christ."[73]

In judging the role of Pilate in the trial of Jesus, we must carefully distinguish between the part Pilate actually played and the one he plays in the gospels. As the highest authority, and the one who alone could impose a death sentence in this period, Pilate had ultimate responsibility and power to make the final decision. He passed sentence of death on Jews; accordingly, Jesus was executed in Roman fashion, by crucifixion. But Pilate was undoubtedly not wholly responsible; according to the gospels, which are probably correct in this matter, the initiative in the arrest and elimination of Jesus came from the chief priests and their Sadducean adherents. There is no indication that Pilate would have proceeded against Jesus on his own; hypotheses to this effect seems quite forced. Although executions without trial are attributed to him, this must certainly be taken with a grain of salt or granted only with restrictions; a Roman official would be quite clear about the extent of his jurisdiction.

In the trial of Jesus Pilate shows that he is anxious, within limits, to follow proper procedure; the limits are to be seen at the point at which major difficulties might arise for Pilate himself. We do not find in him a greater than average commitment to the just cause. Although not exceptionally friendly to the Jews, he would for political reasons have liked very much to do a favor to the Jewish hierarchy, especially if it were to cost him nothing. Against this background, his position and especially his vacillation become understandable.

In the picture given of Pilate in the gospels there is admittedly a tendency to blame the Jews more than Pilate. This is true especially in Luke and, above all, in John. It may be that apologetics are a definite factor in this emphasis. At the same time, however, the evangelists do not whitewash Pilate. Without exception they maintain that Pilate did not help Jesus obtain his just due but instead passed an unjust sentence of death or allowed such a sentence to be forced through.

The Jews bring Jesus from Caiaphas to Pilate's official residence, the praetorium (cf. also Matt. 27:27, Mark 15:16). Many identify the praetorium with the palace of Herod on the west wall of the city near the modern Joppa Gate. But we should rather identify it with the Antonia Fortress at the northwest corner of the temple plaza. Concerning this fortress Josephus says, "Antonia, situated at the junction of two colonnades of the first Temple court, the western and northern, was built on a rock 75 feet high and precipitous on every side. It was the work of King Herod and revealed in the highest degree the grandeur of his conceptions."[74] It was originally named simply Baris (Fortress), but Herod gave it the name Antonia in honor of his Roman friend, Antonius, the well-known triumvir and friend of Cleopatra.

> Where it [Fortress Antonia] joined the Temple colonnades stairs led down to both, and by these the guards descended; for a Roman infantry unit was always stationed there, and at the festival they extended along the colonnades fully armed and watched for any sign of popular discontent. The City was dominated by the Temple, the Temple by Antonia, so that Antonia housed the guards of all three. The Upper City had a stronghold of its own—Herod's Palace.[75]

The Roman procurator, who resided in Jerusalem primarily at the times of the great Jewish feasts, probably lived in Antonia, since from there he could most easily keep an eye on the temple precincts and control the situation. With the mention of the praetorium the place of judgment is indicated. In John's telling, the trial of Jesus now enters the stage of strict public legality.

Verse 28b gives a brief indication of time: "It was early morning"— a statement that reminds us of the "It was night" in 13:30c. Here, as usual in John, the mention of the time has a deeper significance. The day of Jesus' execution, the day on which the Passover lambs and the true Passover Lamb are slain, the day of victory and fulfillment, is dawning.

Those who bring Jesus to Pilate are not immediately named, but according to John they are in fact the Jews, the representatives of the unbelieving world. Their decision with regard to Jesus has been long since made; their chief concern now is to use the Roman judicial system for carrying it out. They do not suspect, of course, that in the process they are coming to grips once again, in a tragic way, not only with Jesus but with their own decision. They will lay their cards on the table and have to play to the end the game they have started.

The Jews themselves do not enter the praetorium in order not to defile themselves, for they wish to eat the Passover lamb during the coming evening and therefore may not allow themselves to become ritually unclean: "For persons suffering from leprosy, venereal disease, monthly periods, or any form of defilement were debarred from participation, as were the foreigners who came from abroad to be present in large numbers at the ceremonies."[76] "At all events, according to the representation of the Evangelist, the real Passover meal had not yet taken place."[77] According to John Jesus dies on the 14th of Nisan, the day prior to the feast of Passover, and in fact at the very time when the Passover lambs are being slaughtered in the temple. According to John Jesus is the "true Passover Lamb," and this conception, at work in the background, helps shape the way the story of the trial is told: "The world that brings Jesus to Pilate is a world that clings to its law. This is true even in regard to the Passover lamb. . . . The very people who are so concerned with the prefigurative Passover lamb fail to recognize the true Passover Lamb."[78]

At the same time, by their action the Jews make their own position clear: they remain outside. Jesus alone is brought into the praetorium; whether immediately or after a delay is not clear. The spatial location of the Jews has a deeper significance in John's portrayal of the events. Over against the rabble-rousing clamor of the Jews outside is set the majestic, tranquil revelatory discourse of Jesus within. But the position of Pilate is likewise determined by the alternation of coming outside and going inside; the place in which he finds himself each time determines the procurator's attitude. The initial positions are now clearly marked; the stage is set and the proceedings can begin.

Pilate goes out and immediately asks the only question that is urgent from the juridical point of view, "What accusation do you bring against this man?" (v. 29). He remains initially on the objective legal plane. The question makes it possible to go immediately to

51

the heart of the matter, and it soon becomes clear just what the issue is. At the same time, the key to the coming sequence of actions is also provided; that is, the question regarding the basis of the charge, and the impossibility of producing a convincing proof of criminality against Jesus, determine the course of the trial.

The answer of the accusers makes it clear that Pilate was right in starting off as he did: "If this man were not a malefactor, we would not have handed him over to you" (v. 30). Instead of offering a conclusive accusation, they make only an unsubstantiated claim: he is a malefactor. The judgment of the world against Jesus is already determined; sentence has already been passed. At the same time, this first answer shows that the Jews have no solid charge to bring against Jesus. Here the innocence motif is sounded for the first time (cf. 8:46: "Who among you can convict me of a sin?"). Jesus is the innocent one, the just person who is finally condemned to death without cause and executed; John's account will emphasize this point over and over. the whole proceedings thus take on an air of vagueness from the outset; they are left hanging in air. According to John hatred without reason (cf. 15:21-25) is what impels the accusers; during the trial the depths of this hatred will be manifested.

There is nothing Pilate can make of such an accusation. Since the facts are not clear, he seeks to refer the accused back to the Jews: "Take him and judge him according to your law" (v. 31a). Here John is pointing to the fact that the Jews themselves had only a limited judicial competence; they could conduct trials according to Jewish law, they could pass sentences and execute them, but not in cases where the sentence would be death. The expression "according to your law" has a double meaning, as will be seen, for it is this very law that will bring Jesus to his death. Only later (19:7) does it emerge that Pilate is on the right track. In any case, without Pilate's realization, his opening question only provokes the death of Jesus; this is part of the paradox inherent in the situation. Pilate evidently wants to avoid having anything to do with this business, but "it quickly becomes clear that in this matter and in this situation . . . it is impossible to avoid taking a stand."[79]

The Jews ignore the reference to their law, but at a later point will return to it with great vehemence. Here and now they must speak out openly and reveal their true intention: "We are not permitted to put anyone to death" (v. 31b). They want the death of

52

Jesus, and this is the only reason why they bring him before a Roman + 3/6
court. The prior decision that brings them to Pilate is a decision that
Jesus must die (cf. 11:47-53).

This little scene closes with a statement that in the answer of the
Jews a saying of Jesus himself is being fulfilled: "Thus the word of
Jesus was fulfilled in which he had indicated what kind of death he
would die" (v. 32). This statement says several things. First, it recalls
the sayings of Jesus about the exaltation of the Son of man (3:14;
8:28; 12:32, 34). The hour of this exaltation, that is, of the crucifixion
and glorification (as a unity) has arrived. It is in the double meaning
that the sign aspect mentioned here consists. The statement is,
second, an indication that Jesus knew in advance what is now hap-
pening to him. The event does not come upon him as blind fate but
as the destiny assigned him by the Father. Consequently, the statement is also a reference to the voluntary character of Jesus' death
(cf. 10:18).

Now the procurator turns from the Jews, enters the praetorium,
has Jesus brought before him, and addresses him directly: "Are you
the king of the Jews?" (v. 33). This question introduces the key
phrase that will be at the center of the proceedings from now on.

The question occurs, in the same form, in all four gospels (cf. Mark
15:2; Matt. 27:11; Luke 23:2), as does Jesus' answer: "You say it"
(ibid., and cf. John 18:37). But between the question (v. 33) and
the answer (v. 37b) which John has in common with the synoptics,
he adds a lengthy insertion (vv. 34-36), just as in v. 37b he adds an
expansion and interpretation of the answer. Verses 34-36 and
37b-c are in the style of the Johannine revelatory discourse and are
doubtless to be attributed to the evangelist who in them gives a new
interpretation of the kingship of Jesus. In other words, John takes
the catchword "king of the Jews" from the tradition, but gives his ✦
own special explanation of what it means. As Pilate's question shows,
he has accepted the accusation as made by the Jews (cf. also vv. 34-
35). It presupposes that Jesus has been delated as "king of the Jews,"
as a messianic claimant.

In John's presentation the title "king of the Jews" becomes the
decisive hard nucleus of the trial, the central issue on which everything else hinges. Consequently it also becomes the formal principle that determines the course of the trial and its aftermath down
to the crucifixion. In the context, and given the manner in which

53

the title makes its appearance, it also reflects the ambiguity of the situation. Various levels intersect here, since the Jews evidently understand the description "king of the Jews" differently than Pilate does, while Jesus in turn understands it very differently from either the Jews or Pilate. The real issue here is the question of the Messiah and the understanding of messiahship. The charge made presupposes a political understanding of messiahship, whereas the new interpretation which Jesus gives of Messiah according to John, presupposes the Christian confession of faith that Jesus is the Messiah promised by God.

In the New Testament and especially in the gospels the *problem of the Messiah* is a rather complicated one, not only in its application to Jesus but even in regard to its presupposition in the Old Testament and Judaism. From New Testament times to the present day Messiah has been the essential christological title among Christians, since *Christos* (from the Greek verb *chriein*, "to anoint") is simply the translation of the Hebrew *masiah* or "anointed one." Also to be considered, however, is the fact that in primitive Hellenistic Christianity the real meaning of the title *Christos* began to fade at a very early date, so that it soon came to form a unit with the proper name Jesus: "Jesus Christ" or, as still frequently in Paul, "Christ Jesus."

The designation "the Anointed (of Jahweh)" originated in the ritual of anointing with oil, especially of the Davidic king at Jerusalem on the occasion of his enthronement: "This royal anointing is part of the more comprehensive act of enthronement which seems to have been based on a whole ritual with various parts."[80] The designation "the Anointed of Jahweh" thus became a fixed title of the Davidic king of Judah. The Old Testament is also acquainted with an anointing of high priests, priests, and holders of the prophetic office, and even of objects. The prediction of the prophet Nathan was extremely important for the religious legitimation of the Davidic monarchy; in it the prophet says to David:

> When your days have run their course and you rest with your fathers, I will establish as your successor the descendant who springs from you, and I will make his dominion endure. He will build a house for me, and I will make the throne of his dominion endure. I will be a father to him, and he will be a son to me. If he acts unjustly, I will discipline him in human ways with whips and rods. I will not

withdraw my favor from him, as I did from Saul whom I rejected before your eyes. Your house and your kingdom will endure forever because of me (2 Sam. 7:12-16).

The Davidic monarchy was thus given religious approval as a long-lasting dynasty. With kingship went the title "Son of God," which designated a sonship by legal adoption (cf. Ps. 2:7; 72; 110; also Ps. 89).

The development of the concept of Messiah was closely connected with the history of the Davidic-Jewish monarchy. Two factors played an important part in this development. One was the fact that, as seen by the prophtets, the Jewish kings failed to measure up to their religious and ethical commission; the failure led to a desire for the coming of a "new shoot of David" who would truly carry out the commission (on this cf., e.g., Isa. 9:1-6; 11:1-16). The second factor was the termination of the Davidic dynasty at the destruction of Jerusalem in 587 B.C.; this led, in the course of the postexilic restoration, to the expectation that the Davidic monarchy might rise again. In the framework of this expectation the concept of Messiah took on the eschatological (apocalyptic) coloring it has in the time of Jesus.

Religious persecution, political repression, and then the rise of the Hasmonaeans in the second century B.C. led to a real escalation of messianic hopes and projects. In every case the hope was also for the national and political restoration of the Jewish kingdom, and this in a manner as close as possible to the ancient model of the Davidic monarchy. These national and political factors are never absent when Jewish sources speak of the Messiah or the Son of David, even if in other respects the conceptions may differ widely from one another. The Essene community of Qumran, for example, knows of *two* messianic figures, "the Messiahs of Aaron and of Israel,"[81] that is, a "highpriestly Messiah" and a "royal Davidic Messiah."

For large groups among the Jewish people and especially for the Pharisees, the picture that is given of the Messiah in the seventeenth and eighteenth *Psalms of Solomon* was probably typical (the *Psalms of Solomon* is a collection of hymns, probably Pharisaic in origin, from the first century B.C.). Here we read, for example:

Intervene, O Lord!
Let their king arise again,

the Son of David, at the time you have chosen, O God,
so that Israel, your servant, may obey him!
Gird him with might, so that he may crush the sacrilegious
    tyrant!
Cleanse Jerusalem of the pagans, who trample her under
    foot so distressfully!
With wisdom and justice let him drive sinners from the
    heritage
and smash the pride of sinners like earthenware!
With a rod of iron let him crush them entirely,
and with the word of his mouth annihilate the sacrilegious
    pagans!
At his threat may the pagans flee before him!
Let him set sinners on the right path, that their hearts may
    have understanding!
Then he will gather a holy people and rule them justly;
then he will direct the tribes of the people that are con-
    secrated to the Lord their God.

Psalms of Solomon 17, 23-28)

According to this passage the Messiah has a role that is at once
national, political, and religious. Also to be taken into account are
the political activities of the militant members of the Zealot liberation movement, for these too were inspired by messianic hopes.

If we inquire into the position of Jesus in regard to the messianism
of his day, the gospels are unanimous in stating that he clearly
dissociated himself from it. Even a conservative scholar like O.
Cullmann comes to the conclusion that

> the great success of the designation Messiah-Christ is all
> the more remarkable in light of the fact that Jesus himself
> always showed a peculiar reserve in accepting it as a de-
> scription of his calling and person, although he did not fully
> reject it. One might consider it really ironical that the title
> Messiah (Christ in Greek) should have been deliberately,
> permanently connected with the name Jesus. The desig-
> nation even gave the new faith its name.[82]

People today once again like to think of Jesus of Nazareth as "fully
in the camp of the patriots in the Jewish resistance" and to call him
a "Zionist politician fighting for liberation."[83] Nonetheless we must
follow the New Testament witnesses who prove beyond a doubt that

Jesus clearly held aloof from the political messianism of his day. As a matter of fact, Jesus became Messiah due to a political misunderstanding of his person and activity. When viewed in this light, the trial of Jesus before Pilate offers the crucial basis for the application of the concept of Messiah to Jesus; it is in this context of the accusation brought against Jesus as being "king of the Jews" and of his execution on the basis of the accusation, that the messiahship of Jesus has its historical origins.

Another factor is the faith in the resurrection of Jesus. This gave the primitive Church the opportunity of interpreting his resurrection by God as his exaltation and installation in divine glory as messianic king of the final age, in a divine glory that is hidden from the eyes of the world. Thus, at the end of Peter's Pentecost discourse as given in the Acts of the Apostles, we read, "Now let the house of Israel know for certain that God has made him Lord and Messiah, this very Jesus whom you crucified" (Acts 2:36). Here we can glimpse what is probably the oldest conception of Jesus' messiahship: by his mighty action in Jesus on Easter God made him Lord and Messiah. It is not the historical Jesus but only the exalted Jesus who is the Messiah, the Christ. A reflection of the same view is found in the ancient formula of faith which Paul cites (Rom. 1:3-4); it distinguishes two stages: ". . . the Gospel concerning his Son, (a) who according to the flesh [i.e. in his human origin] was descended from David, and (b) who at his resurrection from the dead was installed by the Holy Spirit as Son of God in power [i.e., was made messianic ruler]." It is clear that full messiahship belongs only to the risen and exalted Jesus. The crucified Jesus of Nazareth is the Messiah promised by God: this is a confession of faith that for purely human and historical thinking contains an abiding element of scandal which cannot be eliminated.

In quite varying ways the evangelists read their faith in the messiahship of Jesus back into the period of his earthly life; in doing so, however, they maintained the messianic secrecy. They avoided ever putting the title Messiah on the lips of Jesus himself, simply because this would in fact have been inconsistent with the historical truth. Jesus never called himself "Messiah." He could not have applied the title to himself without having radically altered the meaning of his person and life, as the following verses in John make clear.

Pilate's opening question, "Are you the king of the Jews?" raises the whole complex matter of political messianism. As Pilate puts the question, it contains in fact every possible misunderstanding; it cannot be answered with a straightforward "yes" or "no." Jesus cannot simply accept the ideas which Pilate attaches to the word "Messiah," and therefore he replies with a question of his own: "Do you say this of your own accord or have others told you this of me?" (v. 34). Only when Jesus has first clarified this point will it be possible for him to add the correct answer to Pilate's original question. By means of Jesus' counterquestion the evangelist indicates who is really in control of the proceedings.

Pilate retorts with a question of his own: "Am I a Jew? Your own people and the chief priests have handed you over to me. What, then, have you done?" (v. 35). Pilate is not himself a Jew; it was not he, therefore, who excogitated the accusation. As a matter of fact, the initiative in the proceedings did not come from him. Even to Pilate the formal charge seems inadequate: the title "king of the Jews" is not sufficient by itself to justify a condemnation. Therefore he asks, "What have you done?" Pilate does not want to be dependent on a mere formula, but looks for some tangible legal fact. In consequence of this last question he is forced to conclude the innocence of Jesus.

Now Jesus can voice his own understanding of the terms "king" and "royal power." What he says is in the style of the Johannine revelatory discourse, and is a kind of *solemn proclamation of his kingship*. This proclamation constitutes the internal climax of the trial. It is issued with all desirable clarity, at a moment when Jesus realizes that his earthly career is to end on the cross. From this point on and in this perspective there is no need to fear any further misunderstandings. It is here that the problem of the messianic secret finds its solution.

As revelatory discourse, Jesus' words are, in character and form, a testimony; that is, they are not an admission but a confession or profession which admits of no further material questions. Instead, the hearer is necessarily forced to come to grips, in a radical way, with the person of Jesus and the claim he makes. The testimony itself falls into two parts which are separated by a question from Pilate.

"My kingdom (or: my kingship) is not of this world. If my kingship were of this world, my servants would fight to keep me from being

58

handed over to the Jews; but my kingship is not of this world" (v. 36). Jesus speaks here emphatically of "my reign" (Greek: *basileia*). This is post-Easter language, since the earthly Jesus spoke of the reign of God or of God's reign and kingdom. It was belief in Jesus' exaltation as Messiah that led to the further idea of the reign of Jesus. As Messiah-King Jesus participates in God's reign; here we find once again the typically Johannine fusion of the earthly Jesus and the exalted Christ. The concept of the *basileia* or Jesus' reign and kingdom has an eschatological meaning here too; it is the eschatological reality that advances its claim during the present life of Jesus. A characteristic of this reign or kingdom is that it is not of this world. It is not founded on any human or political concentration of power, but has its origin solely in the sphere of the divine. The categories and practices customary in the realm of human power politics are utterly inadequate for understanding this kingdom of Jesus.

The difference is clarified by a concrete detail which even a Roman accustomed to the workings of political power can understand: the kingship of Jesus is not to be imposed by the mechanisms of worldly power, nor may it be maintained with the help of these. The king of this kingdom has no servants who will use weapons to fight for him. In fact, powerlessness in the earthly human sphere is of the nature of this kingdom. This is meant as a statement of principle, but it also corresponds to the nonviolence and love of enemies which the historical Jesus advocated (cf. Matt. 5:38-48). John has correctly seen that Jesus' renunciation of power is an essential part of his preaching. The rule of God as Jesus proclaimed it is the liberating and saving rule of love which utterly rejects any use of force, especially physical. Therefore it cannot establish itself by forcible means. Any alliance with force and earthly power is a compromise with the preaching and will of Jesus.

Nevertheless, this kingship does extend into the earthly sphere; it is not of this world but it is certainly in this world and voices its claim there. The paradoxical relation between this claim to rule and the utter powerlessness of Jesus is evident. A person of power politics, who thinks solely in terms of political and military relationships of power, can only laugh at Jesus' claim; Jesus can only be regarded as a wretched madman or perhaps as a useful fool. Despite this, however, there is the remarkable fact that, as was made utterly clear

59

in the Nazi period, those in political power have at times been more afraid of the intangible, defenseless power of inner conviction and of the word and the spirit than they have of the power of legions and divisions. They regard freedom of thought and speech as far more dangerous. The power of the spirit is not an empty phrase. When a person stands up for it not just with fine words but with a radical personal commitment and a readiness to make sacrifices, then this utterly different power can greatly embarrass and undermine earthly power.

John's statement is misunderstood, then, when the words "my kingship is not of this world" are interpreted as meaning that Jesus is thinking of a completely nonpolitical reality. It is precisely by reason of its *nonworldly character* that this kingship radically affects the entire political sphere and calls it into question. From the standpoint of this kingship political power with all its resources does not represent a last court of appeal or ultimate ground of intelligibility; from this standpoint the profound weakness even of *ecclesiastico*-political power stands revealed. Thus the trial before Pilate in John involves a showdown with political power as embodied in the state. Concretely the issue is with the Roman state, for this was the state with which Jesus had to deal at that moment.

Political power has always been accompanied by the problem of its justification, legitimation, and metaphysical foundation and explanation. It is also accompanied by the tendency to absolutization, the tendency to make of the state and civil power the final and even absolute authority over people. In the time of Jesus the totalitarian claims of the political power were manifested in the Roman principate as well as in emperor worship and the worship of the goddess Rome; in our day they have been manifested in the terrorist rule of the Nazi regime. The ultimate expression of these totalitarian claims is power over life and death or the *ius gladii*, and the use of fear and terror as means of securing domination. Jesus' statement, "My kingship is not of this world," literally removes the very basis of political power as thus understood. The words "not of this world," which are an emphatically negative way of referring to God and his rule and to people's relationship to God, point to a realm of reality over which the state and its power and mere human power in general have no control.

This is meant quite literally: there is simply no way of controlling

60

it; anything humans can control does not belong to this kingdom. This kingdom is the kingdom of absolute, true freedom where the impossibility of having God at one's disposal also reveals and guarantees the nonmanipulatability and freedom of people. Thus the reign of God is the real foundation and, in the last analysis, the only true and reliable basis for freedom from the domination of person by person. In the statement, "My kingship is not of this world" (even if it be not historical), John has rightly seen a basic aspect of Jesus' outlook and activity.

Pilate must take Jesus at his word: that he is in fact a king and therefore makes a special claim to royal rule. Anyone who talks of my kingdom, even if it is a kingdom not of this world, must be some kind of king! Therefore Pilate asks, "You are really a king, then?" Jesus answers, "As you say, I am a king. For this was I born and for this did I come into the world: that I might bear witness to the truth. Everyone who is of the truth hears my voice" (v. 37). To which Pilate answers, "What is truth?" (v. 38a).

The form of Pilate's question, "You are really . . . ?" underscores the unusual nature of such a claim by a defenseless prisoner in this situation. Jesus' answer is intended as a confirmation: "Yes, I am a king." But the concept of king is so transformed by the interpretation following that Pilate is clearly unable to grasp it. This is not to say that such an interpretation was entirely alien in terms of the historico-cultural background. Plato had insisted that either philosophers must be kings or kings philosophers, a view which the Stoics later adopted and advocated. Against this background the concept of a kingdom of truth was quite intelligible. The novelty here is that John connects this idea with the concept of Messiah and thus with the person of Jesus. Jesus is in fact the king of the final age, and this in the manner which he here indicates when he says that the content and purpose of his having been born and come into the world is that he might be a witness to the truth.

In saying this Jesus gives expression to the meaning and purpose of his mission and indeed of his entire existence. The words, "that I might bear witness to the truth," are John's way of stating the fact and manner of revelation. Jesus is the witness to divine truth (for it is this that the word "truth" signifies here) and revealer of God in the world. In his word and testimony God manifests his claim on humanity. It is as revealer that Jesus is king, because he lives entirely

61

by the truth and communicates it. In the encounter with him people experience divine reality as liberating, redeeming love.

But who belongs to his kingdom? "But who is 'of the truth'? Potentially and by destiny all men. In actual fact, however, those who acknowledge and accept their new origin, namely, Jesus and the truth."[84] Whether or not a person is among those who are of the truth is decided in the encounter with revelation and its witnesses. Truth in this ultimate sense is not automatically at our disposal, although we are open to the light of truth, since the question of meaning belongs to our very being. But we are able to encounter this truth in Jesus; we can make a decision on the side of this truth. Thus the concept of kingship acquires a new meaning. It is removed from the realm of power politics and transferred to an existential and spiritual plane.

Jesus, then, has borne witness to his kingship and to himself as king. The testimony has also made clear the real issue in these judicial proceedings, namely, Jesus' claim to be king because he is witness to the truth. Here the real nature of the proceedings is laid bare: they are the action of the cosmos against revelation. The world is putting the witness to divine truth on trial.

The claim of this witness to the truth is also directed against the representative of the state, Pilate the Roman procurator. By the fact that he accidentally must handle the case of Jesus, he too is confronted with a decision. He can bring the trial to its objectively justified conclusion only if he is prepared to surrender his pretension to be a disinterested, neutral, tolerant judge and yield himself to the religious claim of the truth. If he avoids this issue, then the negative outcome of the trial is already decided in principle.

Pilate's famous question now follows: "What is truth?" It has been interpreted in very different ways. Is Pilate here the sceptic and typical representative of Roman reason that has no interest at all in the question of truth? We must ask what objective meaning his question has. It probably means, first of all, that Pilate has no knowledge of the truth and, second, that he evades the claim of truth and therefore the whole question of truth, and puts off his decision. He takes refuge in a refusal to decide. This refusal to decide exactly describes, of course, the existential place Pilate occupies in John's presentation. It will gradually turn him into the pliant instrument of the Jews.[85] At this point the outcome of the proceedings is already decided.

JESUS AND BARABBAS (18:38b–40)

This scene in John is noticeably curtailed in comparison with its presentation in the synoptics. But the curtailment is also a compression. There is no explanation of how the incident came to pass at all. The only motivation for it is the reference to a custom, a regular practice. It is important, however, for the Johannine understanding of the scene to note that it is introduced by Pilate's declaration of Jesus' innocence: "I find no guilt in him." This is followed by the two references to "setting free," which indicate the procurator's desire to let Jesus go free. Finally, there is the contrast between the "king of the Jews" and a murderer. Thus it is clear that the innocence of Jesus is the main motif of this episode.

The interrogation is finished. The question, "What have you done?" has led to no result that can be handled juridically. Pilate should now release Jesus without delay, and this he could have done had he been open to the claim made by Jesus. Instead he turns again to the accusers and tells them of the result of this questioning: "I find no guilt of any kind in him." But why does he not set Jesus free? Because he has refused to make a decision. This is clear from the very fact that he turns now to the accusers and leaves the decision up to them—the worst thing he could do in the situation. They are to decide what is to be done with Jesus.

To this is added Pilate's provocative question, which he evidently intends as ironic: "Do you want me to release the king of the Jews to you?" This brings the idea of Messiah back to the center of the debate. The Jews must now decide how they stand on Jesus, the king of the Jews, and thus on the concept of Messiah. The reaction to Pilate's question is the unhesitating cry of the cosmos, "Not this man but Barabbas!" The scene ends with the laconic observation, "Now Barabbas was a murderer (or: brigand)." The term "murderer" (or "brigand"; Greek: *lēstēs*) is the regular one in Josephus for the members of the Zealot movement. The Romans regarded them as political criminals. John is thus apparently saying, "The Jews reject Jesus, the messianic king, and prefer the politico-messianic gang leader. The criminal who notoriously fitted the description in the charge against Jesus and deserved crucifixion is set free, while the innocent witness to the truth, the religious Messiah, is crucified."[86] Perhaps the evangelist saw in his imagination scenes from the Jewish war, or possibly he thought to himself, "Reject the true king, and you will have a criminal for king."

SCOURGING AND MOCKING OF JESUS (19:1–3)

Unlike the synoptic writers John has incorporated this scene into the course of the trial, perhaps because he is thus able to lend a crescendo effect to his presentation. The internal objective focus of this scene is again the king motif. The stylistic device of role exchange is also used here and in what follows. Pilate has Jesus scourged; this was frequently a part of such proceedings. The purpose of the step here is this: Pilate wants to placate the enemies of Jesus to a certain point, while hoping thus to save Jesus from the worst. From a juridical point of view Pilate's action is arbitrary, since he is convinced of Jesus' innocence.

In the episode of the mocking John agrees chiefly with Mark 15:16-19 (compare Matt. 27:27-30); thus there is no mention of the reed with which the soldiers strike Jesus. The purple cloak is to be understood as a royal robe, even if it is placed on Jesus as part of a parody: *Jesus is invested and enthroned as king, in order that he may receive his first homage.* On this Thomas Aquinas says,

> They showed him insincere homage by calling him king. In so doing they were alluding to the charge laid by the Jews who claimed that he had made himself king of the Jews. Therefore the soldiers paid him the threefold homage due to a king, but did it insincerely, by giving him first a mock crown, second a mock robe, and third a mock greeting. . . . For it was customary at that time, as it still is today, for people coming before a king to greet him. . . . They struck his cheek to show that the homage they were paying him was a mock homage.[87]

The soldiers' actions are a perverse imitation of a royal ritual, here the ritual of investiture and coronation. Jesus received the insignia of his royal dignity, a crown of thorns and a purple cloak, and then the first homage, *Ave, rex Judaeorum!* ("Hail, king of the Jews!"). To sum up: this is how the world regards the kingship and royal claim of Jesus.

ECCE HOMO (19:4–7)

Pilate leads Jesus out before the Jews (v. 4). As John describes it, Jesus had evidently remained inside the official residence while the choice was being made between himself and Barabbas. The presentation to the crowd that now takes place is clearly connected with the previous scene: the invested and enthroned king is now presented to the people in order that he may receive his first homage from them, the acclamation of the people. This too was part of the fixed royal ritual, and John makes use of it in a paradoxical and almost macabre way. We must regard the action of Pilate as a *praesentatio*, a regular royal epiphany. Here the paradox becomes extreme: Never, in all probability, has a king been thus presented to his people and thus greeted by them.

The incident is introduced by the procurator's words, "Look, I am bringing him out to you . . . ," which rouse a solemn expectation. They announce the appearance of Jesus before the waiting throng. The purpose of the action is also given, as Pilate for the second time declares Jesus innocent. By bringing Jesus out, Pilate intends to show that he regards him as guiltless. His purpose is not to appeal to the pity of the crowd but to show that the accusation is groundless. To this end he brings Jesus forth as a wretched and brutally punished king of fools; this is a point that the evangelist deliberately emphasizes. At no moment of the entire trial are we to forget that this person, though not a political Messiah, remains the true messianic king and witness to the truth. Thus we have at this moment a new climax in John's dramatic account.

There is an air of solemnity about the account at this point. The witness to the truth and true king of the Jews makes his appearance before the world. He wears the insignia of a king. He is indeed a "caricature of a king,"[88] but he is nonetheless true king of the world. The scene has the character of a royal epiphany. Even the formula of presentation is not omitted: Pilate presents him with the words *Ecce homo*, "Look at the man!"

It is difficult to give an adequate translation and interpretation of these words. What does Pilate mean by them? Hardly, "There you have the man!" We should probably start with the outward appearance of Jesus, who cuts such a wretched figure before the eyes of his enemies. Perhaps we may think here of Isaiah 53, especially verses 2-3: "He had no beauty and nobility of form, and none of us paid attention to him. His outward appearance did not please us. He was scorned and avoided by men, a man full of suffering and well acquainted with grief. We ostracized and scorned him as one from whom men hide their faces." "In very truth, such a man it is who asserts that he is the king of truth! The declaration *ho logos sarx egeneto* has become visible in its extremest consequence."[89]

Or are we to see in the *Ecce homo* a reminiscence of the title Son of man? It is probable that in the mind of the evangelist the *Ecce homo* has a meaning that lies beneath the surface, and from the context *homo* seems to be more significant than even the title king. But the only higher title than king is Son of man. If this is what is meant, then we have again a paradoxical reversal: The Son of man and world-ruler is without qualification to be identified with this wretched fellow who is brought before the crowd as a king of fools. Grasp that if you can!

Just as a newly crowned king is acclaimed with a joyful greeting when he appears before the people, so here (v. 6) the king is greeted by his people. But what a greeting! "Crucify him! Crucify him!" are the words the Jews spontaneously yell out when they catch sight of him. They are set not only against this king but against this man; that is, they show their inhumanity. At the same time, their shout reveals how sinful people react to the divine reality as it encounters them in the man Jesus. Pilate is angered by the violent reaction of the crowd. He evidently had not expected such opposition after taking this step. Only thus can we explain his words, "Take him yourselves then and crucify him!" since, as 18:31-32 makes clear, this could not be meant as a serious offer to the Jews. In addition, it is clear that Pilate regards Jesus as innocent and therefore wants to avoid condemning him. Consequently, his words must be taken as an expression of indignation and anger: "Take him then and do what you want with him!" Helplessness and irritation cause the procurator to speak as he does.

At the same time, Pilate issues a third declaration of Jesus' innocence. The response of the Jews is an appeal to the law (v. 7), the *nomos;* this they had hyprocritically passed over in silence back in 18:31-32, but now it is brought out into the open: "We have a law." At this point in his *Passion according to St. John* Bach has written music of such intensity that no one who has once heard it will ever forget what the law is.

With these words the religious basis of the Jewish accusation comes to light. That the Jews have the law is a fact which even John acknowledges. Several times in his gospel the Jews appeal to their law (cf. 7:49; 12:34; 18:28). But for John the law is part of the cosmos, not indeed in principle but in fact from the moment when people appeal to it in order to supply a religious justification for their attitude to the revealer. That is precisely what happens here: the Jews appeal to the law in order to justify their demand for Jesus' death. The logic of this law says, "He must die, because he has made himself the Son of God." The law, then, imposes death on the Son of God. The law is dealing, of course, with punishment for blasphemers. In any case, the appeal of the Jews makes one thing clear: piety, as the Jews (the cosmos) understand it in the light of their law, and the revelation of God which Jesus brings are irreducibly opposed. The title Son of God here has its full Johannine meaning.

JESUS AND PILATE (19:8–11)

The final argument the Jews bring forward has abruptly revealed the depths out of which their action against Jesus has emerged. In John's view their motive is hatred of the revealer and Son of God, disguised as an appeal to the traditional norm for Jewish life, the law. According to Galatians 3:13 (cf. 3:7-14) Paul too is of the opinion that the death of Jesus on the cross was caused in the last analysis by the law, so that the human agents involved were really serving the purposes of this legal system when they handed Jesus over to death. This view undoubtedly has its justification; when any legal system is absolutized the result is always inhumanity and injustice, as we are told in the well-known adage, *Summum ius, summa iniuria* ("The supremacy of law is—or becomes—the supremacy of injustice").

In dealing with John we must, of course, take into consideration that the development of faith in Christ along quite different lines than a piety based on the law is an accomplished fact. But we need not assume that John has therefore distorted the facts. If the Sadducees with the chief priests at their head were the real movers in the action against Jesus, they were probably proceeding in the light of their rigorist interpretation of the law. Even Josephus tells us of the harsh sentences passed by the Sadducees.[90] Here, then, they appeal to the God-given law in order to bring about the execution of the human witness to God. This alternative, legalism versus humanity, is prototypical in its significance and has arisen over and over in the course of history. If anyone claims allegiance to Jesus, there should be an awareness of the decisions that will have to be made when conflicts arise.

The argument of the hierarchy did not fail to make an impression on Pilate: "He became even more fearful" (v. 8). Here new light is thrown on the procurator's behavior: he had already been motivated by fear. Fear was at the root of his indecisiveness. There had been something about this business that had made him uneasy from the very beginning. And since he had disdained to seek firm ground in the clear truth offered to him and thus to gain for himself a vantage point that was inherently superior and characterized by an authentic freedom, fear for himself and his life, as well as for his position as a Roman provincial official, gained the upper hand.

The impression of something uncanny about Jesus had forced itself on Pilate at his first meeting with him; it was impossible really to comprehend the man, especially since there were no tangible juridical facts. At the same time, even his positive claim to be witness of the truth was something that lacked any kind of objective status. This impression of Pilate's has now been reinforced by the words about Son of God. Even for Pilate, a pagan, this was a concept that had about it a disquieting aura of numinous power. It is therefore quite logical and typical that Pilate should go back inside with Jesus and feel impelled to interrogate him more closely again (this is an

aspect of the proceedings that is missing in the synoptic accounts).
Thus there is a second conversation between Pilate and Jesus.

The procurator's first question is occasioned by the term Son of
God. He asks, "Whence are you?" (v. 9) and means it to be a
question about the essential origin of Jesus (and not simply about
his place of birth, for example). Pilate wants the kind of information
about Jesus that will make certitude possible. People usually think
they know someone when they know something about that person's
origin or past. Pilate can ask a question like this because his desire
is not to believe but to gain a certainty that is proper to this world.
But Jesus cannot give Pilate the certainty he wants; at bottom there
is no answer to his question but the one Jesus has already given
him in their first conversation (cf. 18:36-37), but Pilate had completely ignored this. The procurator is therefore now disappointed
in his expectation. Since he does not trust the power of truth, he
now seeks support in the truth of power (v. 10): he invokes his
exousia, his authority.

The term exousia refers to the official authority the law bestows
on Pilate, but also to the possibility of its exercise here and now in
a particular case. Pilate is thus invoking the power of office that has
been delegated to him as a procurator of the Roman empire; he
hopes to find certainty and backing in it since it represents a court
of appeal higher than himself and therefore supports him. He is
saying, "Behind me stands the Roman state with its administrative
apparatus, its law, and not least its military power." He mentions
first the authority to set free (the Roman official offers freedom to
the Son of God!) and only secondly the authority to crucify.

To this at least Jesus has something to say in response (v. 11).
His answer is in two parts: (a) it says something about the relationships of power that are operative in the present case; and (b) it speaks
of guilt and responsibility in this same case. Jesus admits that Pilate
has authority and power. But it is not in the nature of this authority
that Pilate can validly apply it against Jesus. His power over Jesus
is given to him from above. The point here is not, as is sometimes
claimed, to give a theological basis for the authority of the state.
The words of Jesus cannot be understood as equivalent to the well-
known principle that all authority is from above, from God. The real
point is rather to indicate the limits of all civil power. Pilate, the
Roman official, is here being set right. His role in this case is

69

salvation-historical rather than constitutional. This possessor of civil power who is quite aware of the jurisdictional limits on his exercise of power, is blind to the power of God and the freedom of the witness to the truth. Worldly power (and this includes the power of the Church as well as of the state) has no control over revelation.

The second part of the answer is now clear. Pilate has acquired his present role and his power over Jesus not from anything in himself but from the divine plan of salvation and the action of the Jews. His position therefore does not represent a real active opposition to revelation but rather a remarkable blindness. That is why John says that the guilt of the Jews is greater. The statement, "Therefore he who handed me over to you is more guilty," represents the reflection of the evangelist and his tradition on the question of guilt in regard to the execution of Jesus. It is probable that in the primitive Church people asked, "How was the guilt shared at that time? Who was chiefly responsible for the death of Jesus: the Jews alone? The Romans alone? Both equally? Both, but the one group more, the other less?"[91]

A critical examination of the sources suggests to me that the best answer is this: Ultimate legal responsibility for the crucifixion of Jesus belonged to the Romans, and if the proceedings led to a judicial murder (and objectively that may very well have been the case), then in this regard the Roman procurator played the decisive role. He was bound to observe the law, and in passing judgment he should not have let himself be moved by the accusation. But it is impossible to absolve the Jewish side, and specifically the dominant Sadducean party, of a *share in the responsibility* and therefore of moral guilt. For they took the initiative in the entire business by arresting Jesus and handing him over.

John's formulation, then, is not incorrect but it does call for some nuancing. In any case we should not overlook the fact that John by no means absolves Pilate of all guilt and responsibility. When he says that the guilt of the Jews is greater, he undoubtedly implies that Pilate too had his full measure of guilt, but a lesser measure. We must be careful in reading the often oversimplified statements of the New Testament and must introduce needed distinctions. Sweeping explanations are of little help. There is no question but that Christians of earlier times passed far too simplistic a judgment on the Jews, and this was disastrous. But we should not therefore make the opposite mistake today and represent every charge against the Jews of that day as Christian apologetics or anti-Jewish polemics.

If Jesus were not the founder of Christianity but simply one Jew among many contemporaries, it would be easier to admit that in his time many other Jews were badly treated by the Jewish aristocrats in power and then handed over to the Romans. The Jewish upper class was, politically speaking, very much in cahoots with the Roman authorities, and many Jews, including Jesus of Nazareth, became the victims of this alliance. On this basis it should be possible to come to agreement on the historical facts, at least to the extent of adopting the same standpoint.

The Condemnation of Jesus (19:12–16a)

Verse 12a tells us that after this final conversation Pilate was evidently seriously determined to set Jesus free, probably because the questionable nature of the entire situation had to some extent become clear to him. Viewed externally, therefore, the outcome might still seem to be fully open. But according to the inner logic of the way the situation was developing the further course of events was already determined.

The Jews see Pilate's intention and now go to every length, including, according to John, the use of political coercion. In so doing they present themselves as more Roman than the Roman procurator. They attack him precisely at the point where shortly before he had hoped to find ultimate assurance, that is, in his official authority: "If you let this man go, you are not a friend of Caesar!" The allusion here is probably to the political title *Amicus Caesaris* ("Friend of Caesar").[92] The Jews were thus putting immense pressure on Pilate, but this kind of manipulation exercised by threatening to lodge a complaint with the emperor—in this case an accusation of high treason—seems to have occurred with some frequency. Blinzler comments, "What a grotesque situation! The highest Roman official in Judea has to endure being accused of lack of loyalty to the emperor by the representatives of a nation more passionately seething with hatred for the Roman yoke than almost any other in the empire."[93]

Pilate had to assume that the Jews would make good on their threat. If he came under suspicion of not having intervened decisively enough against a politically dangerous person, a "king of the Jews," his action could be construed as showing favor to politically subversive forces. In such matters Emperor Tiberius was extremely sensitive.

Pilate now realized the choice he must make, either to condemn Jesus or to open himself to an accusation of high treason at Rome, which would mean the end of his political career. It would doubtless have required an almost superhuman uprightness and an interior independence of an extraordinary kind for a man to be able to resist at this point. This was undoubtedly too much to expect of a Pilate. He is here the prisoner of his own power.

But the Jews too are forced to accept the ultimate consequences of their course. They return to their accusation: Anyone who sets himself up as a king is in opposition to Caesar. The basic motif "king of the Jews" thus remains decisive to the end. But it now becomes clear that the title of king has meanwhile become so linked with the person of the accused that if the Jews are to be rid of Jesus they must abandon even the title of Messiah. First, then, they are forced into a generalization: *Anyone*, they say, who raises a messianic claim is in opposition to Caesar or is, in a real sense, the enemy of the emperor (this is a well-documented form of Roman reason of state). Given the threat of delation, Pilate must yield, whether or not he wants to.

He ceases any further resistance and leads Jesus out into the open once again, in front of the tribunal which he himself ascends in order to give formal validity to his sentence. I regard as unconvincing the (grammatically possible) translation, "He placed him—Jesus— on the judge's bench." For, in John's view, the cross is the throne from which Jesus rules and judges. The point in the present passage is rather that Pilate condemns Jesus in the formally correct manner (*pro tribunali*).[94]

In order to underscore the significance of this moment in the history of salvation John records the place, the day, and the hour. The place is called *Gabbatha* (Greek: *Lithostratos*), which might be translated "Marble Pavement" or "Mosaic Pavement"; the reference is probably to the paved court of Fortress Antonia.[95] The day is the "preparation day for Passover"; this is in keeping with John's Pass-

72

over typology according to which Jesus will die as the true Passover Lamb. The time is "about the sixth hour;" it is midday.

Pilate presents Jesus once again, "Look, your king!" The scene and the phrasing echo 19:5. Although Pilate is yielding he evidently cannot resign himself to being coerced into condemning Jesus; thus his words here are probably bitterly mocking. Or do they represent a final cautious attempt at moving the Jews to withdraw their charge? In any case, it is part of the irony of the scene that this final attempt of Pilate also provides the Jews with a final possibility of taking a stand in relation to Jesus. They react as though they had been touched on a sore spot: "Away with him! Away with him! Crucify him!"

Pilate replies with his final question, "Am I to crucify your king?" It is notable that in this final scene Pilate emphasizes the "your king," thus intensifying the antagonism of the Jews. The gulf between Jesus and the Jews has now grown so wide that it cannot possibly be bridged. The Jews are ready to abandon not only Jesus but even their messianic hope: "We have no king but Caesar!" This statement too can be understood against the political background of the day; the aristocracy doubtless shared the aversion to political messianism and its devotees, not least because these potential kings of the Jews would jeopardize the political power of the aristocracy. A declaration of loyalty to the emperor was by no means unthinkable in the present situation. Thus, according to John, the accusers are dissociating themselves not only from Jesus but from the messianic ideal itself.

Now Pilate has nothing more to gain by appealing to the internal Jewish situation—unless, of course, he were willing to dissociate himself from the emperor. Therefore the trial ends with the words, "Thereupon he handed Jesus over to them to be crucified."

CONCLUDING REFLECTION ON THE TRIAL OF JESUS

In the history with which we are familiar, especially that of the European tradition, there are trial reports which are of such fundamental importance for our historical self-understanding that we cannot imagine ourselves without them. Among such trials would

73

be the trial of Socrates at Athens and the trial of Jesus; at a later period the several trials of La Pucelle, Joan of Arc; nor may we forget the countless trials of heretics, for example, that of John Hus at Constance; and finally the modern showcase trials conducted by the Nazis in their People's Tribunal at Berlin, and so on. Surprisingly, there is, as far as I know, no study in the history of ideas that investigates why these widely varying martyr-trials are so important for our whole way of thinking and living.

A few characteristic traits of these trials may be singled out. Usually the victims are persons against whom no specific crime can be proved; the accusations have no solid foundation, but rather attack certain doctrines or a certain way of life that do not fit in with the generally accepted outlook and ways of life or are even calculated to undermine these in a radical way. The real objection may be to freedom of thought, as in the case of Socrates; it may be to the freedom expressed in the compassionate love that springs from religious conviction, as in the case of Jesus. These are attitudes that create shock waves and have profound consequences. If we look closely, the hatred and rejection by the powers that be at any given time—the Athenian polis or city-state, the chief priests and Pilate—are only too well founded and understandable. The individuals being tried are indeed radicals, not in the sense that they resort to violence, but in the sense that they penetrate to the hidden roots of life, to its real sources—and also to the causes of the prevailing corruption. The death of these persons, however, becomes a beacon of hope for their disciples and for coming generations as well.

To me these trial reports, beginning with the *Apology* of Socrates and the trial of Jesus and coming down to the present day, are among the most thrilling documents we have. They are as it were the hallmark of the human, enabling us to gauge the authenticity but also the cost of true humanness. The person who, though powerless, comes forward as a witness to the truth and dies for it as an expression of ultimate interior freedom, makes clear what is the true meaning of life.

It is precisely the Johannine presentation of the trial of Jesus that shows in a convincing way the relationship between social, ecclesiastico-religious, and political power, on the one hand, and the nonviolent free power of divine truth, on the other. The official Jewish Church of the chief priests and the civil power formed a

74

partnership to destroy Jesus, but this is not the only example of this type of thing. Once the official Christian Church came to power as the established Church, it acted just as its ancestors, the Jewish chief priests, had done. And yet when the defenseless Jesus presents himself as a king and, doubtless with seeming good reason, is mocked as a king of fools, something indestructible, something of a higher order, something not within reach of or even touchable by any earthly power emerges from all this horror and inhumanity, without derogating in the least from the awfulness. That something is the authentic reflection of God in humanity. The words *Ecce homo* hit the bull's-eye! They express the fascinating promise for the sake of which it is possible and good to be a human and love one's fellow humans.

Way of the Cross and Crucifixion of Jesus (19:16b–27)

The trial before Pilate has ended in the condemnation of Jesus: "Thereupon he handed Jesus over to them to be crucified" (v. 16a). Now comes the account of his execution: "Now they took Jesus" (v. 16b). In John it is not quite clear at first who are meant by the "them" (v. 16a; the "they" of v. 16b) into whose hands Jesus is given to be crucified. According to v. 16a it is really only the Jews that can be meant, since Pilate has yielded to their will and condemned Jesus to die on the cross. And yet it is utterly impossible that the Jews should have taken Jesus into their custody and carried out the execution. First of all, crucifixion was a Roman, not a Jewish punishment; secondly, executions were not within the competence of the Jews. Those who took Jesus into their custody can therefore only have been the soldiers of the execution squad (cf. 19:23). It is likely that John deliberately speaks with a certain vagueness here in order to saddle the Jews with an even greater burden of guilt.

For the rest, we get the impression that in recounting the crucifixion of Jesus as reported in the tradition available to him John has deliberately omitted a number of details. It is evident that his account has frequently condensed an earlier and more detailed narrative, with the result that, as here in 19:16, there are clearly places where a poor scissors-and-paste job has been done. In order to bring out more distinctly the special character of the Johannine passion narrative we shall here again bring in the synoptic parallels for comparison.

In a well known and much quoted speech (*Pro C. Rabirio* 5, 16) delivered at a politically inspired criminal case in 63 B.C. Cicero says:

> When death finally threatens, we want at least to die in freedom. Let the executioner, the hooding of the head, and even the very word cross be outlawed not only from the body and life of Roman citizens but even from their thoughts, eyes and ears. For all these things are unworthy of a Roman citizen and a free man.[96]

H. W. Kuhn rightly observes that it is usually only the words about the cross that are quoted. But Cicero is also expressing horror at any capital punishment carried out by an executioner as compared, it is clear, with a free death, that is, suicide; he is also horrified, therefore, at the thought of crucifixion.

> These sentences of Cicero the defense lawyer also express the esthetic judgment of a man who belonged to the equestrian class which was strictly differentiated from the masses of the people and even from the Roman citizenry generally and was made up of gentry with large estates, officials, and holders of leases from the state. . . . It is the chief orator of Rome who here seeks to protect Roman citizens from crucifixion.[97]

At the same time Cicero's words express disdain at the thought of crucifixion since this was the *servile supplicium*, that is, the typical Roman punishment used for slaves and, in the provinces, for real or supposed rebels.

Mark and the synoptic tradition (Mark 15:20b-30 par. Matt. 27:31c-44; Luke 23:26-43). In vv. 20b-21 of his account Mark briefly describes the journey to the place of execution and includes mention of a man named Simon, from Cyrene, being forced, as he came in from the fields, to carry the cross behind Jesus, probably because Jesus was so weak from the scourging and all that had happened to him up to this point. Mark also mentions the names of Simon's sons, Alexander and Rufus. This information may be taken as trustworthy even though it is not mentioned elsewhere. Matthew (27:31c-32) follows Mark closely but has already omitted the names of the two

76

sons. Luke (23:26) likewise mentions Simon of Cyrene as carrying the cross, but he is clearly stylizing the reference for edification when he says, "They laid the cross on him, and he carried it behind Jesus." Simon here becomes the symbol of the follower of Jesus. As a true disciple he carries the cross behind Jesus and follows him on the way of the cross.

Luke has also added a longish section to the account of the way of the cross (Luke 23:27-31). According to him quite a large crowd, chiefly of women, followed Jesus, lamenting and weeping for him. To these people Jesus says, "Daughters of Jerusalem, weep not for me! Weep rather for yourselves and your children! For, look, days are coming when they will say, 'Happy are the barren, whose bodies have not borne children, and happy the breasts that have not given suck.' Then they will say to the mountains, 'Fall on us!' and to the hills, 'Cover us!' For if they do these things in the green wood, what will they do in the dry?" This insertion may originate with Luke the evangelist who is here linking the execution of Jesus with the destruction of Jerusalem in A.D. 70.[98]

The image of "green wood and dry wood" evidently means that if they behave so evilly toward Jesus, an innocent man, as to crucify him, what will they do to those who are in fact guilty? Luke probably has in mind the Jewish leaders who are responsible for the death of Jesus. He evidently regards the destruction of Jerusalem as a divine punishment for the death of Jesus, a conception that was to become widespread among Christians. Eusebius, for example, writes, "It was indeed proper that in the very week in which they had brought the Saviour and Benefactor of mankind, God's Christ, to His Passion, they should be shut up as if in a prison and suffer the destruction that came upon them by the judgement of God."[99] This is an approach that we can no longer accept today without qualification.

Mark says that the place where Jesus was crucified was called *Golgotha,* that is, "Place of the Skull" or simply "Skull" (Mark 15:22 par. Matt. 27:33; Luke 23:33). "According to the evangelist's interpretation of it the name must be from the Aramaic *golgolta, gulgulta* = 'skull.' " The name was probably given because "the bare rock-formation reminded people of a skull."[100] Since it was a place of execution, Golgotha was situated outside the city wall but "close to the city" (19:20).

The data given [on Golgotha in the New Testament] are consistent with the present localization (which goes back to the time of Constantine) in the Church of the Sepulcher at Jerusalem where, about 40 meters from the tomb of Christ, stands a 4.50 meters-high mound that is said to be the hill of the cross. Modern scholarship regards this mound as probably, though not certainly, identical with the historical Golgotha.[101]

According to Mark (15:23 par. Matt. 27:34), before Jesus is crucified he is offered a drink: "And they gave him wine spiced with myrrh, but he refused it." In Mark 15:36 we read again that a soldier gave the crucified Jesus vinegar to drink from a sponge on the end of a reed. With this account compare Psalm 69:21-22: "The disgrace breaks my heart and makes me ill. I wait to see whether anyone will have pity, but there is no one; I wait for consolers, but I find none. They gave me gall to eat and vinegar to drink for my thirst." This verse of the psalm doubtless exercised a strong influence on the way the account is phrased, but this need not mean that the incident was invented out of whole cloth. Blinzler comments:

A narcotic drink, wine mixed with myrrh, was offered to Jesus too when he arrived at Golgotha, presumably by Jewish women and not by the Roman soldiers for it was, as we have seen, a Jewish custom—but He refused it (Mark 15:23). He wished to endure with full consciousness the tortures which lay before Him (cf. also Mark 14:25).[102]

The fact, however, that the same incident is reported twice does cause difficulties.

Mark's account of the crucifixion itself is extremely concise: "Then they crucified him" (v. 24a). Next, the clothing of Jesus is divided: "They divided his clothing by rolling dice for it" (v. 24b). This verse too shows the influence of a verse in the psalms; in Psalm 22:19 we read, "They divide my clothing among them and cast dice for my garments." "According to ancient custom, the executioners had the right to what was left by the executed person."[103] This is probably correct, and the soldiers are hardly likely to have come to blows over the few effects left by Jesus. Here again, however, the important thing is the idea that even such a commonplace and unimportant detail as the division of the executed man's effects is to be seen as a fulfillment of the Scriptures and is therefore presented in the language of the psalm,

There follows (in Mark 15:26) an indication of time: Jesus was crucified "about the third hour," that is, about nine o'clock in the morning. According to John, Jesus was condemned to death only "around the sixth hour," that is, about twelve noon; this is probably closer to the historical reality.

We are also told, "The inscription of the charge against him read, The King of the Jews" (Mark 15:26 par. Matt. 27:37; Luke 23:38). In Mark it is not quite clear where the inscription with the reason for the execution was affixed. Was it on the cross, over Jesus' head? That is how Matthew interprets the situation: "And over his head they indicated in writing the reason for his death: This is Jesus, the King of the Jews." Luke visualized things in the same way. But the inscription on the cross remains quite puzzling.

Blinzler, who on this point harmonizes the accounts excessively and treats them as completely historical, says that "the contesting of the historicity of the inscription on the cross is one of the wilder aberrations of criticism."[104] But, as a matter of fact, apart from the case of Jesus as described in the New Testament, there is no reference in ancient literature to a custom of attaching to the cross over the victim's head a piece of writing that indicates the reason for his death. Consequently there is very little likelihood that a different procedure was followed in the case of Jesus. On the other hand, we are told quite often that it was customary for someone to go before the condemned man on the way to the place of execution, carrying a tablet that indicated the crime.[105] In any event, there can certainly be no doubt that Jesus was condemned to death as "king of the Jews," that is, as a messianic pretender and rebel against the Roman state, and it may well be that a tablet indicating the cause, "King of the Jews," was carried ahead of Jesus. But we may doubt that this tablet was then affixed to the cross over Jesus' head and that, as John claims, it was written in Hebrew, Latin, and Greek (19:20).[106]

Mark reports that two robbers (or thieves) were crucified along with Jesus and placed at his left and right (Mark 15:27 par. Matt. 27:38; Luke 23:33b). The fact as such is not historically impossible. For the two need not certainly have been criminals, that is, robbers or murderers, in the ordinary sense which these terms had in criminal justice; rather, as the Greek word *lēstai* suggests, they may have been Zealots or members of the Jewish liberation movement. In addition, we must reckon here, once again, with the language of Scripture, and specifically with Isaiah 53:13 where we find in the song of the suffering servant the following words: "Therefore I will give him multitudes for his portion, and many shall he receive as his booty, because he surrendered his life to death and was counted among the transgressors, though in fact he was carrying the sins of many and taking the place of evildoers." The passage is explicitly cited by Luke (22:37). The primitive Church, then, saw a connection with the prophecy; in its eyes, the fact that Jesus, the just and innocent one, was executed alongside two criminals was a fulfillment of this passage of Scripture. Throughout the passion narrative we repeatedly come upon the same phenomenon of the primitive Church finding in Scripture, and taking thence, the language in which it could talk about the suffering and death of Jesus.

As a result, we also find the claim repeatedly made by exegetes that the use of this language causes a whole series of events to be invented in order to provide a proof from Scripture. According to this view, because of the descriptions given in Psalms 22 and 69 and in Isaiah 53 the later writers arranged the events so as to fit the prediction. This is undoubtedly too simple a view. There are indeed cases in which because of passages in the Old Testament certain incidents are made up out of whole cloth in order to have a fulfillment. We will find this kind of thing in John too. But it is fairly easy to see through such inventions. In general, however, we must rather distinguish between what actually happened and the manner in which it is reported or repeated, or, in short, between the event and the stylized communication of it. In dealing with the gospels there is this inherent difficulty, that we have practically nothing with which we can directly compare the accounts. Historically speaking, much may have happened as Mark reports it. And as long as there are no decisive reasons to the contrary, we must start with the assumption that his account is fairly reliable.

From the outset, then, the sacred language of Scripture was used to promote the believer's interpretation of the facts. The desire, especially in the story of the passion, was for a sacred history, a history of salvation, and not a mere commonplace list of incidents.

In this approach, the events were lifted to a higher plane, to a literary level on which from the start the focus is on the hearer's or reader's intimate participation and personal involvement. It would be a mistake to take this literary stylization as a direct reflection of historical fact.[107] Before we pass judgment on the historical probability of an account, we must take into consideration the special literary character of the texts.

Luke's addition (in 23:39-43) shows how the scene with the two thieves could be developed in the interests of edification. According to Luke one of the two thieves reviled Jesus, but the other received insight into his own guilt and believed in Jesus, so that he said to him, "Jesus, remember me when you come into your kingdom." Jesus answered, "Truly, I tell you: this very day you will be with me in paradise." All this is not historical fact but a form of proclamation that even a criminal, if he believes, will find salvation through Jesus.

Up to this point in Mark there has been simply one statement of fact after another. Now, however, Jesus is mocked in an episode that is developed at some length (Mark 15:29-32 par. Matt. 27:49-53; Luke 23:35-36, 39). The mockery reflects, once again, a typical element in the psalms, especially in those that are laments of the persecuted just person. For example, "But I am a worm and no man, mocked by men and despised by the people. Anyone who sees me reviles me, screws up his mouth, and shakes his head: 'He trusted in Jahweh; let Jahweh deliver him, let Jahweh rescue him, since he is favorable to him!' " (Ps. 22:7-9; cf. 109:25: "I have become a mocking to them; they see me and shake their heads").

In the description of the mocking we must allow for extensive compositional work by the evangelists; it is very unlikely that the mocking of Jesus by those beneath the cross, or even by the chief priests and scribes, took this form. It is rather to be conjectured that Mark is here making use of current objections to the new faith in Messiah Jesus, as the disciples of Jesus encountered them from the outset, that is, from Good Friday on. The point that emerges with unusual clarity here is that the early followers of Jesus were fully conscious of being in an unpleasantly ambiguous position over against Jewish and later on public opinion because of their belief in one who had been crucified.

In this regard the use of the expression "to be ashamed" in connection with the Christian kerygma is quite revealing. Thus Paul says, for example, "I am not ashamed of the Gospel, for it is the saving power of God for everyone who believes—Jews first, then Greeks" (Rom. 1:16). We cannot help asking why Paul should express himself in this manner; were there perhaps reasons for being ashamed of the Gospel? As a matter of fact, there were, and they had to do with the Gospel as the message of the cross or with the foolishness of the kerygma. "While the Jews call for signs and the Greeks seek after wisdom, we preach a crucified Messiah [Christ] who is for the Jews an intolerable stumbling block and for the pagans sheer folly" (1 Cor. 1:22-23; cf. 1:18-25). Similarly we read in Mark 8:38 (par. Matt. 16:27; Luke 9:26): "For anyone who is ashamed of me and my words before this adulterous and sinful generation, of him the Son of man will be ashamed when he comes in the glory of the Father with his holy angels."

A person is ashamed of what makes him appear in a questionable light to others and especially to society, or makes him uncertain of his own role in society. This kind of social insecurity must have been felt initially by those who accepted the message of the cross; the term "be ashamed of" points to an early period in which the contradiction between the message of the cross and Jewish or pagan society must still have been keenly felt. As people became more accustomed to the message, and especially once Christianity was more fully integrated into society, the sense of this contradiction became weaker and weaker. As early as John the awareness is no longer as keen as it had been.

The mocking of Jesus gives full expression to the contradiction, "Ha! Destroyer of the temple and rebuilder of it in three days! Save yourself! Come down from the cross!" Or, "He saved others, himself he cannot save! Let the Messiah, the King of Israel, come down from the cross now so that we may see and believe" (Mark 15:29-32). Can a man who is hanging on a cross, unable to save himself, be the savior of Israel? A crucified Messiah had no place at all in traditional Jewish conceptions of the Messiah. There is already a certain blunting of the contradiction when Luke shows a thief breaking with the official rejection of Jesus and confessing him to be a just man from whom he hopes for salvation as the moment of death approaches. Matthew, on the other hand, retains the opposition in all its sharpness when he adds to the mockery as recorded in Mark,

"He trusted in God; let God save him now, since he is pleased with him! After all, he said, 'I am God's Son'!" (Matt. 27:43).

The description in John. This gospel is an especially striking example of the extent to which the way that a story is told can become a means of interpretation. There is no room in John for a mockery of the crucified Jesus such as we have seen in Mark. It does not fit in with his conception of the victory and glorification of Jesus. For John the cross is so brightly illuminated by the exaltation of the Son of man that there is no room for anything but the opposition between Jesus and his unbelieving enemies. Believers, for their part, are so fully on the side of Jesus that they no longer feel the opposition. In John's view the cross cannot be a *skandalon* or stumbling block; it is rather the sign of faith's victory.

This is a view that has its dangers, and we cannot overlook them. Admittedly, by means of his own special approach to the passion as the story of Jesus' victory, John is able to bring to light aspects of the passion that emphasize the cross as the revelation of divine love. But in reducing the element of contradiction and *skandalon*, of the real suffering, failure, and downfall of Jesus, John gives support to an idea that was inevitably to prove politically ominous at a later time: the cross, in the form of the *crux gemmata*,[108] of the noble, gilded, sacralized and even fetishized cross, became a sign of rank and honor (cf. the various decorations and medals) in a so-called Christian world! Jesus had died as a man who was one of the oppressed and was accounted a criminal. Now he was being claimed, especially by those in the ruling classes, as legitimation of their spiritual and worldly power! The holy sign of the cross was now perverted in many ways and, in the real life of society, all too often had nothing to do with the authentic cross.

CRUCIFIXION; INDICATION OF PLACE;
CRUCIFIXION OF THE TWO THIEVES (19:16b–18)

The execution squad takes Jesus into its custody. John is careful to observe that Jesus "carried his cross himself and went out to the spot called 'Skull Place' or, in Hebrew, 'Golgotha' " (v. 17). John evidently wants to show that Jesus remained in full possession of his powers to the very end; this is why the figure of Simon of Cyrene, the cross-bearer, does not appear on the scene. John's presentation

83

here seems to be a deliberate correction of the synoptic picture. Jesus is being turned into a hero.

As regards the place of crucifixion John is in full agreement with the synoptic tradition; the spot is Golgotha or Skull Place. The actual act of crucifixion is dealt with very briefly: "There they crucified him and with him two others, one on each side and Jesus in the middle" (v. 18). The two men executed with him are not further described; they will appear once more at the end (19:32). It is not clear what significance these two men crucified with Jesus have in John. The main point seems to be that Jesus hangs in the middle between the other two, a position that emphasizes his special dignity. The center is the place of honor and therefore suited to high-ranking persons. Since the crucified Jesus is king of the Jews, the two men suffering with him seem to be, in a more than external way, attendants at the throne of Jesus and are therefore not described as thieves.

THE INSCRIPTION ON THE CROSS (19:19–22)

We have already said something about the historical aspect of the inscription on the cross; the historical fact of such an inscription may with good reason be doubted. It is therefore all the more important to grasp its symbolic meaning, especially in John. John knows the tradition but has once again made it serve his theological purpose. The king motif which has already played a key role in the proceedings before Pilate is here picked up again and developed further.

John and the synoptics are in agreement on the basic point of the tradition, namely that an inscription attached to the cross explained the reason for the sentence: "King of the Jews." But John interprets this tradition in his own manner when he turns it into a final subject of disagreement between Pilate and the Jews. It is as though the two parties cannot rid themselves of this mysterious, alien prisoner even after he has been executed; he continues to haunt them.

Mark speaks of an *aitia,* that is, a written cause of or reason for death; in other words, the inscription repeats the death sentence by giving the decisive reason for it. John, however, speaks of a *titlos;* that is, he speaks quite generally of a public inscription or notice that is put into three languages: Hebrew, Latin, and Greek.

84

The intention of the evangelist is clear: for him these are the three languages that were chiefly spoken throughout the *oikumenē* or inhabited earth that was coextensive with the ancient world. These are the languages of the entire world to which the crucified Jesus will now be present as revealer and redeemer. The entire world is to realize that Jesus was condemned and executed as "king of the Jews" or Messiah, and that this was not a mere coincidence but corresponded to a deeper truth. The addition of Latin and Greek underscores the fact that Jesus no longer belongs solely to the Jews but to all of humankind. That is the point of John's telling of the incident.

The Jews, of course, are not satisfied with the inscription. Their leaders lodge a protest with the procurator. They want to make Jesus alone responsible for the inscription; that is, the inscription should not read, "This man is the King of the Jews," but should make the point that Jesus gave himself this title or arrogated it to himself. Possibly John also wants to show that the Jews objected to the formulation because if its objective meaning were accepted as true, they would continue to be defined by relation to Jesus. In addition, the inscription on the cross seems to be, in John's eyes, a proclamation of Jesus as king before the entire world. We used to read in the Good Friday liturgy: *Regnavit Dominus a ligno:* "The Lord reigns from the wood" (i.e., from the cross).

On this point, however, Pilate refuses to give in to the Jews. Now that the sentence has been passed he has regained his self-confidence. With his lapidary response, "What I have written I have written," he almost acquires in John the dignity of an unwitting evangelist who by means of his inscription on the cross introduces the public proclamation of the crucified Christ to the entire civilized world of the time.

THE DIVISION OF THE GARMENTS (19:23–24)

Here again John is in agreement with the tradition when he tells of the soldiers of the execution squad sharing the effects of Jesus. But if we are correctly to understand John's interpretation of the incident we must take as our starting point the passage of Scripture which John sees as being fulfilled.

In the synoptic gospels this passage is merely echoed, but in John

85

it provides the basic framework for the telling of the incident. Just as in the story of the entry of Jesus into Jerusalem (Mark 11:1-10 par.) a citation from Scripture (Zech. 9:9 = Matt. 21:5) causes the one ass in Mark to become two in Matthew (Matt. 21:2: "You will find an ass and a colt with her"), so here the citation from Scripture causes John to depict the division of the clothing as taking place in two stages. The soldiers act in a way that corresponds perfectly with the verse of the psalm. To the first part of the verse there corresponds the division of the garments; to the second part, which must also have its fulfillment, there corresponds the casting of lots.

It is natural to conclude that the seamless tunic is an invention of John who is inspired to it by the scriptural text. It is possible that the evangelist has something special in mind when he introduces this feature and that later interpretations (which begin in the Fathers of the Church) to the effect that the seamless tunic refers to the unity of the Church are not entirely false. However, the clearer of these two motifs in John is that of the fulfillment of the Scripture, which, in his view, must take place in a literal way. Precisely in his account of the crucifixion of Jesus we get the impression that the entire series of events takes place in undisturbed and exact accordance with a plan foreseen by God and Scripture. The evangelist is careful to record each incident, so that by comparison with Mark's account John's is characterized by a strict orderliness. Therefore at the end of the scene we read, "That, then"—i.e. what the Scripture foretold—"is what the soldiers did."

THE WOMEN BENEATH THE CROSS (19:25)

In keeping once again with the tradition (cf. Mark 15:40-41; Matt. 27:55-56; Luke 23:49; cf. also Luke 8:3) John tells us of women beneath the cross. The next little passage will also mention the "disciple whom Jesus loved."

The New Testament traditions are not in full agreement on which women were present at the crucifixion of Jesus. In Mark 15:40-41 we read, "There were also women present, looking on from a distance; among them were Mary Magdalene and Mary the mother of James the Lesser and Joses, and Salome, who had followed and served him when he was in Galilee, and many other women who had gone up to Jerusalem with him." Matthew repeats Mark but rearranges the names (Matt. 27:55). He makes the observation that many women stood beneath the cross of Jesus, among them Mary Magdalene, Mary the mother of James and Joseph, as well as the mother of the two sons of Zebedee, with whom the Salome mentioned by Mark is identified (cf. also Matt. 20:20). Luke in turn sees the scene a little differently: "All his friends, including the women who had followed him from Galilee, were standing at a distance and watching" (Luke 23:49). The names of the women of whom Luke is speaking here had already been given earlier (8:1-3) in a short summary of Jesus' activity in Galilee. They are, "Mary, called the Magdalene [i.e., the woman from Magdala], from whom seven demons had departed, and Joanna the wife of Chuza, one of Herod's officials, Susanna, and many others."

There is only one name that appears in all these lists: Mary Magdalene. The agreement of Mark and Matthew is clear enough; the few changes in Matthew are not very important. It is likely that some women from the company of Jesus were present at the crucifixion; Mary Magdalene was most probably one of them. John is the first to mention Mary, "the mother of Jesus." Although this became part of the tradition (cf. the well-known hymn *Stabat Mater dolorosa*, "The sorrowing mother stood"), the historical critic must raise a number of questions about it. Since John wants to show that the death of Jesus took place in an orderly way, the mother of Jesus could not be absent; so too the disciple whom Jesus loved had to be present. Here again we can perceive a clear tendency in John to suppress disturbing and unpleasant elements. The death of Jesus must be marked by a certain glorious splendor.

In addition, the women stand beneath the cross "as representatives of those who believe,"[109] in contrast to the soldiers.

The Testament of Jesus (19:26-27)

Hardly any passage in the story of the passion as told by John has been so much discussed or been the object of so much puzzled speculation and interpretation as this short narrative.

We will do well to interpret the account in the light of its immediate context in the gospel of John and, in the beginning at least, to avoid speculations that range beyond the text.[110] We must start, then, with the fact that these two verses are not only material pe-

87

culiar to John in this context, but are in addition a Johannine development. Dauer offers the following reasons for this assertion: (a) the synoptic accounts of the passion record no words of Jesus to any of his kin nor do they say anything about the presence of Mary or any male disciple beneath the cross; (b) the predictions of Jesus about a flight of the disciples tell against the presence of one of them beneath the cross; an especially cogent point here is that in 16:32 John shows himself aware of the tradition of the general flight of the disciples and is therefore to some extent contradicting himself.[111]

In all likelihood, then, we must attribute the entire scene to the evangelist himself. In Dauer's view,

> this is not to say that he invented the entire scene out of whole cloth. There is no reason for doubting that Jesus made some provision for his mother when he realized how precarious his own situation was. Moreover, it is not unlikely that he gave care of her to a disciple who was especially close to him. The evangelist, however, *changes the place and time of this action* of Jesus and introduces it into the scene of the crucifixion.[112]

This is a conjecture that may possibly explain the facts, but we really know nothing about what happened, and it is highly doubtful that we should make a working hypothesis of such a conjecture.

In any case, most of the difficulties and misgivings arise in connection with the mariological interpretations of the text that were commonly given at an earlier time and that sought to deduce from it a special role for the mother of Jesus, and specifically a universal mediatorship. The mother of Jesus is mentioned only three times in the gospel of John: at the wedding feast of Cana (2:1-11); in 6:42, where we read, "Is this not the son of Joseph, and do we not know his father and mother?"; and finally in the present text. It is notable that John always speaks only of his mother and never mentions the name Mary. The mode of expression is very unspecific and stereotyped, and we must therefore ask whether the fourth evangelist really had any precise knowledge about the mother of Jesus at all. If he did, then at least he has not passed it on to us.

A further consideration is that John, especially in the story of the wedding feast of Cana, shows the relationship of Jesus and his mother as marked by a great sense of distance, a kind of estrangement. Although people avoided admitting this in the past, there can

88

hardly be any doubt that the answer of Jesus to his mother's remark, "They have no wine," amounts to a rather brusk rejection: "What has that to do with you and me, woman? My hour has not yet come." Jesus the revealer and his mother have no human level in common.

In 6:43 the name of Joseph is mentioned but not that of Mary. In the scene beneath the cross the relationship seems to be somewhat more positive, since Jesus makes provision for his mother before the end. But here again, as the address "Woman" (instead of "Mother") shows, the distance has by no means been eliminated. The real point seems to be this:

> The words of Jesus have the sound of a final testamentary disposition; that is, the point is a kind of "provision" made for "those left behind" in either a natural or a transferred sense. But for whom is Jesus here making provision: for his mother or for his disciple? The most obvious interpretation is that as a son who is taking his farewell Jesus makes provision for his mother who is remaining behind.[113]

According to Exodus 30:12[114] the law imposed on a son the duty of caring for his mother. Jesus can no longer carry out this responsibility; therefore he bequeaths this duty to the disciple whom he loved, making him his representative: "According to the law a woman's male relatives must always provide for her. This is the responsibility Jesus entrusted to the disciple who was his favorite."[115] Jesus wants everything to be in good order as he dies. This is the interpretation Thomas Aquinas offered long ago,[116] and J. S. Bach introduces it into his *Passion according to John:* "He made good provision for everything in his final hour; / he kept his mother in mind still and gave her a guardian. / O man, do justice, which is beloved of God and men; / then die without grief and be not saddened" (no. 56, Chorale).

The figure of the disciple whom Jesus loved is not further identified in this account. It is said only that he stands with the others beneath the cross; possibly his function here is also that of witnessing, to which express reference will be made in 19:35. From the viewpoint of the text it seems only natural in a way that this disciple whom Jesus especially loved should accept the responsibility of caring for the mother of Jesus.

But does the scene not have a deeper, more symbolic meaning? R. Bultmann writes:

Doubtless this scene, which in the face of the Synoptic tradition can make no claim to historicity, has a symbolic meaning. The mother of Jesus, who tarries by the cross, represents Jewish Christianity that overcomes the offence of the cross. The beloved disciple represents Gentile Christianity, which is charged to honour the former as its mother from whom it has come, even as Jewish Christianity is charged to recognize itself as "at home" within Gentile Christianity, i.e. included in the membership of the one great fellowship of the Church. And these directions sound out from the cross; i.e. they are the commands of the "exalted" Jesus. Their meaning is the same as his words in the prayer, 17, 20f., the request for the first disciples and for those who come to faith through their word. . . .[117]

This view of the text has rightly been criticized. It is true enough, of course, that in reading John we must allow for a symbolic meaning to the scene, but we must also base the symbolism on the whole of Johannine theology and not reduce it to a bright but exotic idea dragged in from outside.

V Schürmann observes:

> There should be no need of proving that in the "spiritual gospel" of John the "last words" of the crucified Jesus, which are given such telling prominence, are not meant to refer solely to earthly provision for Mary but have a further significance. After all, the other narrative elements of the crucifixion scene, which provides the immediate context, are full to overflowing with meaning.[118]

Here is Schürmann's own interpretation:

> The disciple whom Jesus loved stood beneath the cross as witness to the tradition behind the gospel of John (or even as its author). In the person of Mary all those who expect salvation from the Exalted One and who are willing to receive his word are committed to the care of the witness and thus of his gospel. On the cross Jesus declares this gospel to be "canonical" as it were and binding on the Church. In this way the "Exalted One" from his place on the cross creates the unity of believers through all ages by having his commissioned "disciples" pass the word on (see John 17:20-21). . . . By means of this final directive, which is pre-

sented as effectively operative, Jesus knows that the "work" which the Father had "assigned" to him (17:4) is "completed" (cf. 4:34; 19:28, 30; cf. 5:36; 14:31). The formation of the one Church by means of the word is the crown of the earthly "work" of Jesus.[119]

This explanation seems at least plausible, since it is based on facts and tendencies verifiable in John. It is questionable, however, whether so much emphasis should be laid on the idea of the unity of the Church, which seems to be expressed rather in the seamless tunic.

In interpreting the passage we must start with the fact that this testament of Jesus indicates first of all his definite departure from his own. Jesus is leaving his own behind in the world, and among these are his mother and the disciple whom he loved. This means, of course, that everything Jesus said in the farewell discourses about his departure is also applicable here. At this moment his words are being fulfilled: "And yet I tell you truthfully: It is to your advantage that I should go away" (16:7). His death is a condition for the existence of the community of disciples in the world, so that from the Johannine viewpoint this testament of Jesus would be concerned with what might be called the establishment of the community of Jesus.

At this point we should in all likelihood look back to the very beginning of the farewell discourses in chapter 13. There the washing of the feet was a symbolic, anticipatory representation of the death of Jesus as a death springing from a love unto the end or unto completion. It is this "unto completion" of 13:1 that is picked up again in 19:28-29: "Since Jesus now realized that everything was completed. . . . " Consequently, verses 26-27 must be taken as an expression of this completion; that is to say, Jesus, the Exalted One, from his place on the cross establishes the community of his own by referring Mary and the disciple whom he loved to one another for all time to come, in a relationship in which they symbolize and represent all of Jesus' disciples. Here again, therefore, the commandment of love is given visible expression: "I give you a new commandment, that you love one another; just as I have loved you, you must also love one another" (13:34). Hoskyn is right when he comments, "The Church proceeds from the sacrifice of the Son of God, and the union of the Beloved Disciple and the Mother of God prefigures and foreshadows the charity of the *Ecclesia* of God."[120]

If we go back now and review from this vantage point the sequence of scenes that make up the Johannine account of the crucifixion, we can perceive an inner theological connection between them. Verses 16b-18 begin by indicating the fact and location of the crucifixion of Jesus. In verses 19-22, which recount the dispute over the inscription on the cross, the refusal of Pilate to alter the text causes the kingship of Jesus, which has emerged during the trial, to be definitively asserted before the world (cf. the three languages!). The division of the garments (vv. 23-24) fulfills the Scripture, and to the letter, but at the same time points to the unity of the community of Jesus. The final section (vv. 25-27) depicts the establishment of the community of Jesus beneath the cross; this community, which is symbolized by Mary and the beloved disciple, is bound by the commandment of love unto the end as well as by the commandment, "Love one another."

The Death of Jesus (19:28–30)

The description of the death of Jesus in John turns logically into a description of his victorious end.

The key theological word that describes the death of Jesus in John is "complete" or "accomplish" or "fulfill" (Greek: *teleioun*), which occurs three times in this passage. Jesus knows that everything is now completed or accomplished. This knowledge is the knowledge the revealer has of his own way and of the task he was to fulfill. Verse 28 states in lapidary fashion that this task is now finished. There is left only the fulfillment of the Scripture which says, "They gave me gall to eat and vinegar to drink for my thirst" (Ps. 69:22). John takes the Scripture text and its fulfillment from the tradition (cf. Mark 15:36) but, since he is speaking in this context about completion, he is saying that this incident also finishes the fulfillment of the Scriptrures, or that this process of fulfillment too is complete.

In any case, the text and its fulfillment are located in a different framework in John than in Mark. According to Mark 15:34-36 Jesus cried out "in a loud voice": "*Eloi, Eloi, lama sabachthani*—My God, My God, why have you abandoned me?" This gave the bystanders the mistaken impression that he was calling on the prophet Elijah for help. "One of them ran and soaked a sponge in vinegar; he put it on a stick and reached it to Jesus to drink from. As he did, he said, 'Let us see whether Elijah will come and take him down'" (cf. Matt. 27:46-49). In Mark (and Matthew) the horror and pity of Jesus' death is heavily emphasized. The death is signaled by the coming of a great darkness, a kind of cosmic grief, as it were; the terrible deed that the death of Jesus represents is shrouded in deep night.

Then there is the abandonment of Jesus by God. It is incorrect, in the view of Mark at least, to deduce that because Jesus here utters the opening verse of Psalm 22, which ends in thanksgiving and praise (Ps. 22:23-32), his words are not an expression of abandonment by God but that he is rather looking forward confidently to victory. That is certainly not what Mark intends to say, as is made clear by the misunderstanding, "He is calling on Elijah . . ." and by the remark, "Let us see whether Elijah will come and take him down." There is no miracle in Mark nor any halo of glory around the death of Jesus. Jesus dies with a loud cry. Only then do various signs occur: the tearing of the curtain in the temple and the confession of the centurion, "Truly this man was a son of God" (Mark 15:38-39).

Matthew has added further signs (27:51-53) according to which the death of Jesus has an eschatological significance: it introduces the eschatological turning point of the ages and therefore the general resurrection of the dead. Luke's presentation follows its own line, for it emphasizes the submission of Jesus to God to the very end. According to Luke the final words of Jesus are: "And Jesus cried out in a loud voice and said, 'Father, into your hands I commend my spirit.' After saying this he died" (Luke 23:46).

The tendencies in the post-Markan interpretation of Jesus' death are easily recognizable. It is possible even at this early date to speak of a tendency to turn Jesus into a hero. In Mark Jesus is abandoned by God and dies a wretched death; he ends with an inarticulate cry, and this description probably comes closest to the historical fact. In Luke the death of Jesus is portrayed as the death of a just and pious man, the death of the Savior who continues to welcome sinners to the very end and then commends his soul to God.

93

In John the death is that of the revealer, the royal witness to the truth, who continues to the end to complete his work in obedience to the Father's will. The death of Jesus is the eschatological victory over the cosmos and its ruler. Abandonment by God has no place in such a picture. The man who dies here is one who is bringing his work to completion, even in the final instructions he gives from the cross. Therefore everything must be aureoled by the radiance of the fulfillment that is now breaking through. Thus the final words of Jesus in John are quite to be expected: "It is completed." These words are the seal and signature to the entire work of Jesus and to his revelation of God which attains its climax in this death that is the perfection of love.

The Piercing of Jesus' Side (19:31–37)

This narrative is peculiar to John and probably "of a relatively late origin."[121] There are no links here with the synoptic tradition. It is no longer possible to say with certainty whether or not the Johannine text reflects special traditions based on historical information. On the other hand, the allusion to the "curse on the hanged man" (Deut. 21:21-22) is also to be found in Paul (Gal. 3:13) and may reflect very early anti-Christian polemics. Even the reference to the fact that the one who vouches for the incident was an eyewitness (v. 35) is not very conclusive, since in this episode the real intention of the evangelist operates once again at the level of theological statement.

These theological concerns are easily recognizable. The evangelist wants, first of all, to document the fact of Jesus' death. Secondly, he apparently intends to make a symbolic statement that relates to the Church. Thirdly, he intends once again to point out that the Scripture has been fulfilled, and in connection with this to establish a Passover typology. The two Scripture citations at the end give the key to the entire incident.

The account begins by saying that even after the death of Jesus the Jews endeavored to go on applying the law to him in all its strictness. The reason for this is evidently the fear that the hanged man may pollute the entire land, especially on the greatest of the feastdays. In the background is the law: "If a man has committed and you hang the dead man on a post, the corpse is not to remain a crime for which the punishment is death, and if he is executed on the post overnight, but you are to bury it on the same day; for a hanged man is cursed by God. You shall not defile the land which the LORD, your God, has given you as your inheritance" (Deut. 21:21-22). The prescription originally referred to a person who was hanged, but it was later extended to one who was crucified. We may compare here a short passage in Flavius Josephus who says in connection with the murder by Idumaeans of the high priest Ananus and a man named Jeshua, "So devoid of decency were they that they threw out the dead bodies without burial, though the Jews pay so much regard to obsequies that even those found guilty and crucified are taken down and buried before sunset."[122]

Here, as so often, John shows his familiarity with Jewish ideas and customs. He explains the action of the Jews by a reference to the Preparation Day. In his view Good Friday was doubly a preparation day: for the approaching sabbath and for the solemnity of Passover; this is why the text speaks of a high sabbath day.

The Jews therefore ask Pilate to inflict the *crurifragium* or "breaking of the legs" on all three of the crucified men. This was a punishment that could be inflicted independently, but which here is evidently meant to hasten death if it has not already occurred.[123] Pilate issues a command to this effect, and the soldiers carry it out on the two men crucified with Jesus. "But when they came to Jesus and saw that he was already dead, they did not break his legs, but one of the soldiers drove a spear into his side, and immediately blood and water ran out" (v. 33). Blinzler comments:

> Then the Roman soldiers came and killed the two thieves by breaking their legs with an iron club. They did not do this to Jesus when they saw that he was already dead. But in order to make sure that he would not still have a spark of life left in him when he was removed from the cross, one of them drove a spear into the area of the heart. The flow of blood and water showed him that death had in fact already occurred.[124]

This comment refers to only one aspect of John's statement, namely the evangelist's desire here to provide an irrefutable proof of the death of Jesus.

As a matter of fact, the thrust of the spear is introduced less in

95

order to make sure that Jesus was really dead than "in order that the Scripture might be fulfilled"—even though this may strike the modern reader as odd. The blow with the spear is a symbolic action, and it is this aspect of it that chiefly interests the evangelist. The interpretation that has been customary since the time of the Church Fathers and relates the action to the sacraments of baptism and the Eucharist is still better founded than any ingenuously realistic explanation. The symbolic character of the piercing is clear above all from the fact that in John's gospel the wound in the side is an important characteristic of the risen Jesus (cf. 20:20, 25-26); in other words, it is a sign of the exalted Jesus.

> The evangelist chooses his words carefully here, for he does not say: "He struck his side" or "wounded it" or anything similar, but "he opened" it, so that the door of life was as it were thrown open there and the sacraments of the Church flowed forth without which there is no entering into the life that is true life. That blood was shed for the forgiveness of sins; that water is mixed in the cup of salvation, and provides both bath and drink.[125]

At this point there is a reference to a witness: "And he who testified to this was an eyewitness, and his testimony is true; and he knows that he tells the truth, in order that you also may believe" (v. 35). The reference to the witness is meant to underscore the trustworthiness of the account, and there is no reason for doubting that the evangelist is appealing here to an informant and his clearcut testimony. However, the Johannine concept of witness is not limited solely to the external and factual but includes elements of the situation that in the last analysis are accessible only to faith.[126] The witnessing is of a definite kind for which it is not enough to have seen something factual; the witness must also have seen the fact as a revelatory event, that is, in its theological significance. It is a testimony based on faith and capable in turn of awakening new faith. We may assume without further ado that in a general way this testimony of faith goes back to the original circle of witnesses to Jesus and that the otherwise unknown informant of the evangelist may have belonged to that circle. How far the testimony matches the historical facts is another question and one that may be left open.

There follows a reference to the fulfillment of two passages of

Scripture: "They shall not break any bone of his" is a reference to Exodus 12:26 where it is said of the Passover lamb, "You are not to break any bone of it."[127] In John's mind there is doubtless a Passover typology here: Jesus is the new, true, eschatological Passover Lamb for Christians. With Christ a new order of things (the new covenant) becomes effective. Paul had already said, "Sweep out the old yeast; you are without leaven. For Christ our Passover Lamb has been sacrificed. Therefore let us celebrate no longer with the old yeast, the yeast of malice and wickedness, but with the unleavened bread of purity and truth" (1 Cor. 5:7-8). That Christ is our Passover can hardly have been a specifically Pauline idea but represents rather a conception already present in the tradition of the pre-Pauline communities.

The second passage of Scripture reads, "They look upon him whom they have pierced through, and they lament for him as men lament for an only son; and they weep bitterly for him as men weep bitterly for a firstborn son" (Zech. 12:10b). In Zechariah the one who is "pierced through" is a figure shrouded in mystery, and the interpretation of the passage is much disputed.[128] In Horst's view:

> Thus we must view the death of the one man in connection with the destruction of the many, the persecutors, and we should probably think of the prior death of the one man as being the cause of the destruction of the enemies. . . . We should think of the one man's death as sacrifice of expiation an innocent man makes in order to rescue others from affliction by enemies . . . , and the allusion may come from an eschatological myth not otherwise known to us.[129]

For John Jesus is the one "whom they have pierced through" and to whom all will now look for salvation (cf. also 3:14-16). He plays this role as the one raised up or exalted, who (as we have already mentioned) in his risen state still carries the marks of his wounds as permanent signs of his humanness, suffering and death. Whoever looks upon him obtains salvation and life; whoever ignores him brings judgment on himself.

This final scene on the cross thus fits perfectly into the framework of the Johannine theology of Jesus' exaltation. Even the final episode of the passion signifies a final glorification of Jesus; even the soldiers who pierce Jesus through with a spear are serving a hidden divine intention: namely, to show that this crucified man is the savior of the world and the way to salvation for all.

The Burial of Jesus (19:38–42)

All four evangelists report that after his death on the cross Jesus was taken down from it and buried (Mark 15:42-47; Matt. 27:57-61; Luke 23:50-56; John 19:38-42). Despite the undeniable plausibility of these stories of the burial, they offer great difficulties from the historical viewpoint and from the viewpoint of tradition-history.[130] We should therefore be cautious about drawing direct historical conclusions, although the possibility of a speedy burial cannot be excluded. We should bear in mind that from a literary point of view the stories of the burial are not to be interpreted without reference to the subsequent accounts of Easter; the burial stories prepare the way for a number of features in the Easter accounts. As applied to John, this means that since according to his report the burial of Jesus is done in full accordance with the law and includes the anointing of the body (which represents an explicit and irreducible contradiction of the synoptic accounts) he does away with an important reason for the coming of the women to the tomb on Easter morning.

With regard to various individuals features of the accounts J. Blinzler notes[131] that according to regulations the bodies of executed persons belonged to the Roman state, which regarded the refusal of burial as an additional punishment or dishonor. The release of an executed person's corpse could be obtained only by an act of administrative clemency which depended on the pleasure of the competent magistrate. When relatives asked for the release of the body, this was usually granted. Emperor Augustus especially seems to have yielded to such petitions as a rule. Judaism for its part attached very great importance to burial, in the family tomb if possible, but this honor was refused to those who had been executed. For such persons there were two public burial places, one for those who had been stoned or burned, the other for those who had been beheaded or strangled. Sinners were not to be buried in the neighborhood of the upright, lest the latter be dishonored.

As depicted by the evangelists, the burial of Jesus seems to take place within the general framework just described. But the initiative

98

is not likely to have come from the Jews, as John claims,[132] since then the body of Jesus would certainly have been thrown into the common grave for criminals; Joseph of Arimathea would have been too late with his request. The whole account is an insertion that is clearly incompatible with the traditional story of the burial.

According to Mark's account (15:42-47), which here again provides the basis for the accounts in the other two synoptic gospels, the initiative for the burial of Jesus came from a man named Joseph of Arimathea. Mark describes him as a "distinguished member of the Council, and one who was also waiting for the kingdom of God" (15:43). He was thus a person who on the one hand was close to Jesus and his movement, but on the other was a member of the Council and thus in a position to have access to the procurator. The figure of Joseph of Arimathea has a fixed place in the tradition represented by the burial stories and is thus an important reason for assuming this tradition to have a historical nucleus, especially since he is someone who is encountered nowhere else and also belongs to a different social class than the disciples of Jesus.

According to Mark the removal of Jesus from the cross and his burial must have been done very rapidly. Evening is close at hand, and the sabbath, on which no work can be done, begins at sunset. Joseph of Arimathea therefore goes in haste to Pilate, who is surprised that Jesus has died so quickly. He receives confirmation of Jesus' death from the Roman centurion in charge of the execution, and then releases the body of Jesus. Then Joseph buys linen, takes Jesus down from the cross, wraps the corpse in the linen, "and laid it in a tomb hewn from the rock and rolled a stone before the entrance to the tomb" (15:46). For the continuation of the story in Mark it is important that there was no time before sunset to anoint the body of Jesus. Important too is the closing remark, "Mary Magdalene and Mary the mother of Jesus were looking on from a distance and saw where he had been laid" (15:47). On Easter morning they will go out to the tomb.

In John (19:38-42) there is no trace of any lack of time or of any haste and consequent omission in the burial rites of Jesus. On the contrary, the burial takes place with all solemnity and with all due care for the body of Jesus. Here again it is Joseph of Arimathea who takes the initiative; John introduces him as a "disciple of Jesus but a secret one for fear of the Jews." Pilate releases the body to him without any ado. Then the body is taken down from the cross. A further personage introduced by John is Nicodemus, "who had first come to him at night" (a reference to 3:1, 4, 9; cf. 7:50). He too belongs to the class of prominent Jews; this can be seen from the fact among others that he contributes the spices—"myrrh and aloes, about a hundred pounds of them"—for the anointing of the corpse.

John's intention is to show that there was nothing lacking to the anointing of Jesus but that everything was available in abundance. Unlike the Egyptians, the Jews did not customarily embalm corpses, but they did anoint them with oil that was mixed with fragrant perfumes.[133] The body of Jesus, then, is anointed and perfumed, then wrapped in linen cloths, "as is customary among the Jews" (cf. the raising of Lazarus in chapter 11, especially verse 44). The point of the remark is that Jesus received a burial which was exemplary as judged by Jewish custom.

The actual burial is described in verses 41-42 and illustrates once again the evangelist's inclination to describe things in as accurate a way as possible. Close to the place of execution there was a garden, and in it a new tomb in which no one had yet been laid: special honor is due to the Son of God even in death. Jesus is brought there. The closing words, "on account of the Preparation Day, since the tomb was close at hand," are probably a faint echo of an earlier tradition or account which, like Mark's, had reported a quick burial. As we indicated, there is no trace left of this haste in John.

THE STORY OF EASTER
(20:1–31; 21:1–25)

Like the other three gospels the gospel of John ends with the Easter message of the resurrection of Jesus. Jesus, the revealer and giver of life, who as incarnate Logos had by his very nature been linked to God, could not be held prisoner by death. Death for him was but a necessary transitional stage on the way to the Father. Once again, therefore, our question here is how did John understand the Easter message which as such was the common possession of primitive Christianity? Where, in his view, is the meaning of Easter to be located? In answering this question we cannot, of course, ignore problems which in our day are seeming objections to the Easter faith.[134]

Contemporary Discussion of the Resurrection of Jesus

In the New Testament tradition about Jesus, death and burial do not have the final word. Instead, it is reported that the disciples subsequently experienced the person of Jesus as newly alive. The message about God having raised up the crucified Jesus—the Easter faith—was from the outset a part of the good news which the primitive community preached to people. Thus in his sermon on Pentecost Peter says, "God has raised up this Jesus: of this we are all witnesses. . . . Let the entire house of Israel know, therefore, that this Jesus whom you crucified has been made by God to be Lord and Messiah" (Acts 2:32, 36). These words are probably the expression of a very ancient tradition (cf. Rom. 1:3; 1 Cor. 15:4).

This message of the resurrection of Jesus is not just a further, basically superfluous appendage to the account of Jesus given in the gospels. Rather it expresses the new relationship which the primitive community and the evangelists were conscious of having with Jesus after Easter: namely, that for them the person and cause or work of Jesus were not over and done with after the crucifixion, but that they themselves were turning out to be pioneers who had the power to initiate a new movement or development.

Thus it was the period after Good Friday that saw the formation of the eschatological community of salvation with its characteristic faith in Messiah Jesus and its formulation and proclamation of the gospel or good news, in which Jesus the crucified Messiah was preached as the son of God who had been raised from the dead, as the Lord and redeemer, and as God's saving act. This same period saw the development of the mission to the Gentiles, the emancipation from Jewish legalistic piety, and, in brief, all the varied impulses that finally led to Christianity's becoming a world religion, a faith whose adherents were to be found in every nation.

There is no question but that according to the testimony of the New Testament writings the originating event which gave rise to all the processes just mentioned, especially the formation of the community and the public preaching of Jesus as Messiah, is very closely connected with the complex that is more or less globally designated by the key phrase "resurrection of Jesus." However one may interpret the Easter faith of the primitive Church, there is no avoiding the problem of this originating event, as we may provisionally designate the fact that after Good Friday the disciples of Jesus experienced a new start. This new beginning requires some satisfactory explanation. The question, then, is: "What took place between Jesus' death and the proclamation by the Church?"[135]

All that went before appears in a new light—new since the *Easter faith in Jesus' resurrection* and founded upon this faith. But if Jesus' person and work appear to them in the light of the Easter faith, that means that his significance lay neither in the content of what he had taught nor in some modification of the Messiah idea. It does mean, though, that *Jesus' having come was itself the decisive event* through which God called His Congregation (Church). It means that Jesus' coming itself was already an eschatological occurrence. Indeed, that is the real content of the Easter faith: God has made the prophet and teacher Jesus of Nazareth Messiah![136]

Moreover, if we have any understanding at all of the religious, social and political impact of the crucifixion of Jesus as seen against the cultural background of the time, one thing becomes clear to us: The simple fact of this crucifixion could not but be an almost insuperable obstacle to any attempt at remaining faithful to the cause of Jesus or entertaining renewed hopes for its future success. From the historical viewpoint, the chances of the Jesus movement continuing after the Master had died in this manner were minimal to say the least. In any case, the attempt to continue preaching the pre-Easter message of Jesus had to reckon with this handicap that could not possibly be neutralized. There could be no question, then, of simply picking up where Jesus had left off.

Divergent responses are given to the question did the execution of Jesus on Good Friday mean a break for the disciples, or was there a continuity that made it possible to establish a community after Easter despite Good Friday? Schillebeeckx has recently defended the second of these two views: "Of course the disciples felt the violent end of their Master's life as a tremendous shock and so, understandably enough, fell because of their 'little faith' into a state of panic; but they did not in consequence of these last events undergo a complete lapse of faith."[137] In his opinion, the break is already "to be located within the ministry of the historical Jesus, in the resistance to him and the rejection of his message."[138] "Even prior to Easter Jesus is saying, in effect at any rate, that the 'Jesus affair' is to go ahead. This is not just a vision born of faith and based solely on the disciples' Easter experience; it is his self-understanding that creates the possibility and lays the foundation of the subsequent interpretation by the Christians."[139]

Schillebeeckx also points to the example of John the Baptist:

> If the exegetes and theologians who start from the death of Jesus as the point of disjunction (and so not from men's rejection of him as the real break) want to convince me in this regard, they must first show me why, when John the Baptist had been beheaded, his movement was able simply to continue on Jewish ground—as if that death had entailed no break at all.[140]

The two cases are not fully parallel, however; there are important differences to which Schillebeeckx evidently does not give sufficient consideration. John the Baptist was executed in the mountain fortress of Machaerus, away from the public eye, at the order of Herod Antipas, the then tetrarch of Galilee. A somewhat lengthy period of time probably elapsed between his arrest and his execution. During this period it seems his disciples could visit him; contact with the outside world was not broken completely (cf. Matt. 11:2-11 par. Luke 7:18-28). This means that the movement he had initiated was being carried on by his disciples, independently of him, even while he was still alive.

In the case of Jesus, on the other hand, death followed much more suddenly upon arrest; moreover, he was executed publicly at Jerusalem, "close to the city." The Jewish authorities collaborated in his execution, which was not the case with John. Jesus was discredited by the religious authorities. Any continuation of his movement must in any event expect to be monitored by the Jewish hierarchy, less so by the Roman procurator.

After death John was not proclaimed to be the Messiah, even though some of his disciples may have pinned eschatological hopes on him. The disciples of Jesus, on the contrary, proclaimed the crucified man to be Lord and Messiah. This proclamation of him as Lord and Son of man made sense only in a Jewish environment. The disciples must have known—and the texts confirm the fact (see above on Mark 15:29-32) that to proclaim, "The crucified Jesus of Nazareth is the promised Messiah," was to expose themselves to public criticism, and this with regard to a central point of the Jewish expectations regarding salvation. In these circumstances people had to be very strongly motivated if they were nonetheless to go ahead with such a proclamation. In other words, in the case of Jesus the conditions in which a new start was made after his execution on the cross were incomparably more difficult than in the case of John the Baptist.

Of course, even if one regards these difficulties as very serious, one must still grant Schillebeeckx that there was no absolute break. "In all his teachings and all his actions he [Jesus] constitutes a continual scandal, which either provokes a spontaneous answer of trust and love or attracts deadly aggression. Before the 'scandal of the cross' comes the 'scandal of Jesus Christ.' "[141] So too the disciples surely did not suddenly abandon their memories of the real Jesus; questions and problems remained, and the disciples must have thought about these and even discussed them with one another. The accounts of the appearances are testimony to this ongoing link with the pre-Easter Jesus, for they describe the encounters with the risen Lord as a re-cognition.

And yet all this does not adequately explain the new beginning that occurred after Easter. It is possible, of course, to figure that the disciples who had felt the impact of the personality of Jesus and of his behavior and activity and thus had themselves experienced the liberating power of his action should go on believing in their teacher's message and should after a while regain their courage and continue to promote the cause of Jesus in their coteries. But it is much more difficult to explain in this fashion how the crucified Jesus of Nazareth could himself become the content of the kerygma or preached gospel. For the point the disciples are making is not that Jesus and his message are valid despite Good Friday but that now Good Friday itself belongs to the substance and main content of the new faith, and this because it is connected with the assertion that God has raised Jesus from the dead.

If Paul can sum up the gospel as *logos tou staurou*, "the message of the cross" (1 Cor. 1:18), it is not because he is a masochist who is trying to pass off pain and failure as a great success. On the other hand, the only reason why he is not a masochist is because the message of the cross is connected with the Easter faith that the resurrection of Jesus represents the beginning of a new creation. In answer to the many attempts to explain the continuity between the pre-Easter and post-Easter situations in a purely historical and psychological way it must be said that these attempts are too vulnerable to the accusation of wishful thinking which seeks to pass off Jesus' failure as a form of success. No, there is need here of a clear theological basis for the continuity.

There is a further point: Precisely because of the Easter faith, the relationship of the post-Easter community of Jesus to its Master is not to be conceived as simply a historical connection with the personality of a founder. Jesus is not only the highest doctrinal authority for the community. The connection with him acquires a here-and-now character, expecially in the liturgy which the community celebrates. Christians understand the Lord Jesus to be a power that is present and operative; they understand him as continuing to direct the community of disciples through his Spirit: "Now the Lord is the Spirit [the *Pneuma*]," says Paul, "and where the Spirit of the Lord is, there is freedom" (2 Cor. 3:17). Easter, then, does not involve simply an extraordinary historical occurrence but a complex reality that is foundational and vast in scope; it involves the ground of faith and of the Church. One way in which people misunderstand Easter is to think of it always in terms of an extraordinary occurrence and to lose sight of its complexity.

R. Bultmann has correctly pointed out that the resurrection of Jesus is not be equated with the "resuscitation of a dead person" and his restoration to life in the present world.[142] Similarly, the Easter event is not a historical event in the same sense that the cross is a historical event in our history. Only the Easter faith of the first disciples can be understood as a historical event.[143] Even in the New Testament the actual resurrection is nowhere described; what is reported are the encounters with the risen Jesus.

These remarks are meant simply as warnings against misunderstandings that are to some extent suggested by the language of the biblical accounts themselves or by the literary genres used in these accounts.

Because the New Testament describes only the encounters with Jesus, present-day exegetes prefer to ask what the experiences were that led the disciples to their Easter faith.

> Belief in the resurrection can never be grounded purely in the claims of authority; it presupposes a faith-motivated experience of renewal, of life totally renewed, within which actuality (and not just a subjective conviction) is affirmed in a very fitting way—an experience in which the Church as a whole—people and leaders—recognizes its own *ker-gyma* and which is in turn corroborated by the faith of the Church.[144]

In order to pinpoint this special experience Schillebeeckx uses the concept of "disclosure experiences" as elaborated in Ian T. Ramsey's philosophy of language.[145] According to Ramsey all talk about God, or religious language in its totality, must be based on a "cosmic disclosure," a comprehensive, all-embracing disclosure experience that communicates an "infinite" transcendental insight.[146] Ramsey thinks that this kind of disclosure experience is very much connected with verifiable facts or perceptible realities which serve as a basis or condition, but that at the same time the experience always goes further or moves beyond the immediately given to a total and comprehensive disclosure of meaning. Both factors—a concrete experiential point of reference and a comprehensive experience of meaning—play a part in the disclosure experience. The latter is related to situations in which there is "something observable plus something more."[147]

It is undoubtedly possible to understand the Easter experience of the disciples as a disclosure experience in the sense described, since in the Easter experience the element of universal, ultimate, eschatological interpretation is just as important as the question of the concrete point of reference for the experience.

In Schillebeeckx's view this disclosure experience takes the form of a *conversion process* which the disciples went through, so that they realized their own paucity of faith and therefore came together again under the leadership of Peter.[148] This conversion process they then interpreted with the help of the appearances and finally by means of the description "resurrection from the dead."

This view of Schillebeeckx has much to commend it, for the disciples certainly underwent a conversion after Good Friday. But the question immediately arises, how and by what agency did this conversion take place? Schillebeeckx speaks of an "event engendered by grace," that is, "the process whereby Peter and his friends were brought together again after their dispersal was felt by them to be an act of sheer grace on God's part."[149]

But this claim seems quite inconsistent in the light of his presentation. Experience of grace replaces something concrete with an abstraction and provides only an apparent explanation inasmuch as it presupposes the very thing to be proved. The decisive point about the New Testament is that it does not speak in this context of an experience of grace or anything similar, but that the experience in question has rather a concrete christological structure: It is the *renewed encounter with Jesus* that alone provides a solid foundation for this experience of grace!

We can, then, fully agree that the disciples underwent a conversion process. But the factor that triggered the conversion was in the last analysis simply the encounter with Jesus as alive. The historico-genetic explanations offered by all the widely divergent interpretive models (these explanations do not in any way help us to bridge the qualitative leap, the break) agree with the New Testament itself in seeing the stimulus for the new beginning after Good Friday as coming ultimately *from Jesus himself.* The Easter appearances say the same; they bear witness to the impossibility of having Jesus at one's disposal but also to his nearness and readiness to help.

107

Moreover, this renewed encounter with Jesus was so profound in nature that the disciples could understand and articulate it only in terms of a resurrection of Jesus by God. We should not overlook the fact that the concept, resurrection of Jesus, says something not only about Jesus but about God as well. The ultimate issue here is our understanding of God. The disciples experienced themselves as being seized by a new spirit and gifted with a new life.

If Easter has the central, comprehensive, eschatological meaning which the New Testament claims for it as a new beginning for Jesus after the end had come, then we must be clear in our minds that from both the theological and the historical viewpoints it is not possible, on objective grounds, to inquire into what lies behind the Easter faith, unless our intention is to dissolve this faith into its supposed elements. It is really impossible to locate any single point at which we might lay hold of the Easter faith as it comes into existence. The New Testament contains quite varied formulations of the Easter faith, but all of them simply describe the new life in a more or less approximative way. Moreover, we must agree with Bultmann when he says:

> We cannot buttress our own faith in the resurrection by that of the first disciples and so eliminate the element of risk which faith in the resurrection always involves. For the first disciples' faith in the resurrection is itself part and parcel of the eschatological event which is the article of faith. [150]

Our purpose, then, is not to remove the risk of faith by getting behind the historical facts and drawing inferences from them, but to share the risk of faith through a proper understanding of the Easter message.

The New Testament Easter Testimonies and Their Significance

The New Testament texts that attest to the Easter faith of the first Christians are difficult to interpret because, as formulas of faith or even as accounts of Easter, they are at the same time always recounting the genesis of the primitive Church and its situation in the early days. They always have something of the myths of origin about them, with the difference that the origin in question does not lie back in the obscurity of prehistory but is a historical origin.

All the texts agree that the Christian community understands its relationship to Jesus of Nazareth not as a relationship to a historical figure but as a relationship to a living present reality, to a person who in many and varied ways determines the present life, thought, and behavior of the community. The experience of the presence of the Lord Jesus Christ takes clear precedence over historical retrospect; in fact, the latter is wholly in the service of the present at each moment.

Simplifying somewhat, we can distinguish three genres of Easter testimonies: confessional formulas, hymns, and the Easter stories such as we find in the gospels. The ancient confessional formulas and hymns are, from a literary point of view, older than the Easter stories; for this reason they are also to be given priority in regard to their content. A mistake that is constantly being made is to combine all the different types of text in a slipshod way in an attempt at historical reconstruction. As far as the Easter stories in the gospels are concerned, we must take into account their kerygmatic character. They do indeed contain historical reminiscences and fragments of tradition, though usually in a radically reworked form, but their main concern is not historical but rather to bear witness to the risen Jesus and his significance for the present.

The letters of Paul provide formulas of faith which Paul had found already present in the tradition of the communities and had taken over for his own use; to some extent he has reworked them in the light of his own theology.

a) The introduction of the Letter to the Romans speaks of God's Gospel

> regarding his Son,
> who according to the flesh is of David's seed
> and according to the Holy Spirit was established
> as Son of God in power since his resurrection from
> the dead. (Rom. 1:3-4)

This text may well be pre-Pauline. It is of interest because it distinguishes two stages or modes of existence for Jesus. The first stage is summed up in the phrase "according to the flesh" (*kata sarka*) and is coextensive with the earthly human existence of Jesus; in this stage Jesus comes "of David's seed" and is regarded as a son of

David. Whether this was historically the case is a separate question. In this context the earthly existence of Jesus as a son of David is seen as a period of candidacy for his messiahship. It is followed by a stage "according to the Holy Spirit." In this second stage Jesus was established as Son of God in the messianic sense as depicted in Psalms 2 and 110. He was established as Messiah "since his resurrection from the dead"; the resurrection of Jesus marked the beginning of his rule as powerful Messiah.

The great antiquity of the formula in Romans 1:3-4 is evidenced by the fact that according to it only since his resurrection has Jesus been established as "Son of God in power," that is, as messianic ruler. According to this conception of things he was not Son of God from the beginning, but only became this after a time. It quickly became impossible for people to speak in this way any longer. According to this text, belief in Jesus as Messiah depends on the Easter faith; this is a connection that probably takes us back to the early Palestinian community. Luke takes a somewhat similar line in Acts 2:32-36.

In the literary formulation of this Easter theology or theology of the risen Jesus various models are at work, but especially Psalms 2 and 110, which are enthronement psalms. It is from these psalms that the designation of Jesus as Son of God comes: "He [God] said to me: 'You are my son; today I have begotten you' " (Ps. 2:7; 110:3). The title Son of God has a *messianic*, not a metaphysical meaning. The community that chose this formulation was undoubtedly well aware that the earthly life of Jesus could not be regarded as a messianic existence. At the same time, the formula in Romans 1:3-4 says that "since his resurrection" Jesus has been enthroned at God's side as messianic ruler (exaltation theology).

b) "He was handed over for our sins and raised up for our justification" (Rom. 4:25).

This formula too seems to be pre-Pauline. It connects the death on the cross and the resurrection, and does so in a characteristic manner. The idea of vicarious expiation and forgiveness of sins is linked to the death on the cross, and the idea of divine justification and therefore new life is linked to the resurrection. The text probably originated in the early Jewish-Christian community; the justification terminology points to this. Justification or justice as the essence of salvation is a typically Jewish concept. In his own doctrine of justification Paul has given the concept an extensive development.

c) The most important formula of faith occurs in 1 Corinthians 15:3-5, although as part of a larger context (vv. 1-11):

> I want to remind you, brothers, of the gospel that I preached to you; and you accepted it and have taken your stand upon it. It will save you if you hold fast to it as I preached it to you; otherwise your faith would be in vain.
>
> The main teaching I handed on to you was teaching I myself had received:
> *that Christ died for our sins in accordance with the*
>   *scripture*
> *and that he was buried*
> *and that he was raised on the third day in accordance with*
>   *the scripture*
> *and that he appeared to Cephas, then to the Twelve;*
> afterward he appeared to more than five hundred brothers
>   at once,
> of whom most are still alive,
> although many have fallen asleep;
> then he appeared to James,
> then to all the apostles;
> last of all, as to one born by miscarriage,
> he appeared even to me.
> For I am the least among the apostles, since I am not worthy to be called an apostle; for I persecuted the community of God; it is only by the grace of God that I am what I am, and his graciousness to me has not been in vain, but I have labored far more than all the others—not I, but God's grace with me. Whether I or they: thus do we preach and thus do you believe.

The two- or four-membered formula of faith, the most important part of which is contained in verses 3b-5 (italicized in the quotation), relates in parallel succession the death of Christ for our sins in accordance with the Scripture, his burial, his resurrection on the third day in accordance with the Scripture, and his appearance to Cephas-Peter and the Twelve. The death and burial of Christ belong together, as do his resurrection and appearance to the disciples. It is not possible to say what knowledge, if any, of the events described in the gospels—burial of Jesus, journey of the women to the empty tomb on the third day or the first day of the week—lies behind this text. If the incidents were known as described in the gospels, this text is at least not especially interested in them. It is more likely, however, that the Easter accounts as we have them represent later expansions of the kerygma.

The memorandum-like conciseness of the formula of faith has often been emphasized; the formula contains a minimum of information or communication and simply lists the various events without any details. Its concision evidently presupposes a good deal of theological reflection; for this reason very close attention must be paid to the choice of words.

The words "he was raised on the third day in accordance with the scripture" undoubtedly posit the resurrection of Jesus as a new fact alongside the statement of Jesus' death and burial. They evidently assert a new action of God in regard to Jesus. There is, of course, no description at all of this action. The new fact is not an independent reality alongside or outside of the proclamation; it figures only within the framework of the text, that is, in the word.

"On the third day" gives a date, but the sense in which it does so is disputed. There may be an allusion to the women's discovery of the empty tomb; or the reference may be to the date of the first Easter apparition, the one to Peter; or the phrase may represent an apocalyptic date, and specifically the time that will elapse, according to apocalyptic thinking, between the final catastrophe and the advent of final salvation.[151] There is something to be said for taking the phrase in this third sense. Furthermore, it is hardly possible to harmonize smoothly the various testimonies regarding Easter. The primitive Church seems to have been unconcerned about such harmony and to have accepted all sorts of inconsistencies; in any event, the substance of the Easter faith is unaffected by such discrepancies. The tradition regarding the "appearance first to Peter" and the appearances to the Twelve shows various points of contact and correspondence but no complete agreement.

The expression "he appeared" (Greek: ōphthē, which can also be translated, "he allowed himself to be seen") has an almost technical meaning. It is noteworthy that according to this idiom the risen

Christ is the subject of the appearing, while those then named are its (indirect) objects. The term is the same one that the Old Testament uses for theophanies.[152] In fact, from the viewpoint of the history of forms, many accounts of theophanies in the Book of Genesis (for example, God's appearance to Abraham in Gen. 18) provide the clearest parallels to the Easter stories.

We may say, then, that the formula of faith in 1 Cor. 15 describes the appearances of the risen Jesus after the model of a theophany. One element in the model is that people cannot force or produce such appearances; the appearances can only happen to them. Another element is the juxtaposition of hiddenness and manifestation: a reality that is totally hidden from people, totally beyond their power to manipulate, makes itself accessible to them and reveals itself to them. The risen Christ possesses this kind of freedom and complete autonomy; "he allowed himself to be seen." We make no attempt here to describe the psychological dimension of this seeing or appearance; the formula tells us nothing about it. Only the content of the appearances can be determined: it is the crucified Jesus of Nazareth who is experienced as the one who "has been raised from the dead." The usual term in the oldest testimonies is "He has been raised" (Greek: ēgerthē), that is, by God; only later does the term "He is risen" (Greek: anestē) also come into use.

Those to whom an appearance was granted are then named. The sequence is probably meant to be chronological: first Cephas-Peter, then the Twelve. The objection that Judas was no longer there and so there can only have been Eleven is a valid one, of course, and in fact the gospels take account of it.[153] The formulation shows, however, that the Twelve formed a fixed circle, probably beginning during the earthly life of Jesus.

Paul also mentions an appearance to "more than five hundred brothers at once," another to James, "the brother of the Lord," another "to all the apostles," and finally adds his own experience of Christ near Damascus as a final appearance that is not in the sequence but nonetheless stands with full right alongside the others. The formula says nothing about when or where the appearances took place; the important thing is the fact of the appearances and— for Paul in the context of the First Letter to the Corinthians—the possibility of being able to refer, in preaching, to witnesses of the risen Jesus and to the consensus thereby established: "Whether I or they: thus do we preach and thus do you believe" (1 Cor. 15:11). All this does not provide an irrefutable proof that Jesus rose from the dead, for the assertion of the resurrection is inseparable from the testimony of the witnesses adduced. If, then, faith requires the acceptance of the resurrection of Jesus, it follows, above all, that this faith can never consist simply in a relationship to a dead past or in the acceptance of a purely authoritarian dogma against all reason. Faith in the resurrection means rather to take the risk of regarding Jesus Christ and his message as a present reality that determines my life and thus my future. By any accounting the Easter faith expresses the fact that Christian faith in Jesus is not a bag of empty formulas but entails my being vitally touched by the person of Jesus.

In the last analysis, a rigid dogmatism with its insistence on the correct orthodox formulas has all too often distorted and even hindered a vital Easter faith. Distressing though the fact may be, it is probably the case that many who believe in the resurrection of Christ in words and according to the book are far removed from any vital Easter faith and that many who regard the Easter faith as an unreasonable demand but nonetheless reckon with Jesus by affirming his basic attitudes and teachings are close to the living reality of Easter. For the Christian Easter faith confesses Jesus of Nazareth to be alive; this faith is concerned, in the last analysis, with the great symbol of unconquerable hope for humanity. When viewed in this light, the resurrection of Jesus is a cosmic disclosure, a comprehensive and permanent source of meaning for people, as we read in the hymn, *In te, Domine, speravi; non confundar in aeternum,* "In you, O Lord, I have placed my hope; I shall not come to naught for ever."

Is it possible to go a step further and say anything about the possible historical course of events? As we have seen, the formula states the fact but provides little basis for historical reconstruction, except to indicate the sequence of witnesses, with Peter being the first to whom the risen Jesus appears. If we want a more detailed picture, we must go to the gospels for help. But in doing so we must be on our guard, since while many ancient bits of tradition are contained in the Easter accounts of the gospels, they have become so much a part of narratives which have been shaped by the evangelists, that it is difficult to detach these elements from their context and from the interpretation this context provides. It is all too easy for later interpretations and even speculations to be given priority, even though these go far beyond what the texts have to say and are often characterized by vagueness. Then there is the further fact that Matthew and Luke are once again basically dependent on Mark, while also adding special traditions of their own.

The first appearance to Peter has left traces everywhere. In Mark the angel who serves as messenger to the women at the empty tomb says, "Go and tell his disciples and Peter: He is going ahead of you to Galilee; there you will see him, as he told you" (Mark 16:7; cf. Matt. 28:7). According to Luke the Eleven tell the two disciples from Emmaus, "The Lord has truly risen and appeared to Peter" (Luke 24:34). John 23:3-10 still reflects this tradition.

Then there are the further appearance stories. Matthew tells us of an appearance of Jesus to the women (Matt. 28:9-10), but this seems to be a later creation of the evangelist. The great Easter appearance to the eleven disciples takes place on a mountain in Galilee (Matt. 28:16-20). This account too has been shaped by Matthew, but there may be in the background a tradition about appearances in Galilee. Luke for his part introduces the story of the two disciples on the way to Emmaus (24:13-35); it may be that the evangelist has made a sublime Easter story out of an Easter tradition that is perhaps now discernible only in the name Cleopas. Luke also transmits a report of an appearance to the eleven disciples while they are at table, links it to a final commission of Jesus to the disciples, and ends with the removal of Jesus from the sight of the disciples (Luke 24:36-43, 44-53).

By and large, except for the stories of the women at the empty tomb, the gospel accounts of the appearances add nothing essentially new to 1 Cor. 15:3-5. But the "more" that is to be found in these stories must be attributed to the evangelists, each of whom is developing his own Easter theology in these texts. From this point of view, of course, their stories are very important.

There is a further point that must be mentioned. According to Mark and Matthew the Easter appearances take place *in Galilee,* as they do in John 21; according to Luke, however, and in John 20, they take place *in Jerusalem.* Luke has even deliberately changed Mark's presentation. In Mark we read, "Go and tell his disciples and Peter: He is going ahead of you to Galilee; there you will see him, as he told you" (Mark 16:7). In Luke, on the contrary, the Easter message of the angel reads as follows, " 'Why do you look for the living among the dead? He is not here, but is risen. Recall how he told you, while he was still in Galilee: the Son of man must be delivered into the hands of sinners and be crucified; but on the third day he will rise.' Then they remembered the words. They returned from the tomb and told all this to the Eleven and all the others" (Luke 24:6-9). It is very likely that Luke has here introduced an alteration in favor of Jerusalem. This very fact is already an argument that the tradition which locates the Easter appearances in Galilee is probably better founded and the more ancient.

The actual fact, then, may have been what Mark indicates. According to him (14:27-28 par. Matt. 26:31-32), when Jesus is walking with his disciples to the Mount of Olives he predicts that they will fall away and flee, "but after my resurrection I will go before you into Galilee."[154] Relevant here is the statement in Mark 14:50 that when Jesus was arrested all of his disciples abandoned him and fled. There is a strong tendency, especially in Luke, to exonerate the disciples, but this is a deliberate alteration to the record and not a better tradition as is sometimes claimed.

This, then, is the historical picture that emerges: According to Mark who in this case is our most reliable historical source, the disciples all fled when Jesus was arrested, and they went back to Galilee; Peter was among them. There they had the disclosure experience which our sources describe with the help of the concept of Easter appearances. These experiences must, at the very least, have been overwhelming religious experiences in which the person of Jesus was central. He came to the disciples in a new way; the disciples realized that not only were they not finished with him but that only now would things really begin to move. A new beginning was being made. In this new beginning in Galilee Peter must in fact have played the leading role. Perhaps it was he who gathered the disciples together again and took the initiative in returning to Jerusalem and forming the community. In addition, there were probably collective Easter experiences (this is where the accounts of the various Easter appearances to a larger circle of people are soundly based).

People are overready to read too much into these brief reports—

until they finally realize that the strength of the testimonies resides precisely in their terseness. For in the last analysis the stories say nothing of any kind of visions and subjective interior experiences. What emerged from these occurrences has proved remarkably enduring. I mean, first, the *common kerygma*: the confession of Jesus, of his person, of his history and his work, and not least of his failure as well; and, second, the community that accepts commitment to his name, celebrates his memorial in the Lord's Supper, and, in the process, experiences his presence and a communion with him in faith and Spirit. To this extent Easter means that *Jesus himself* was acknowledged as God's eschatological act and as the abiding Lord of his followers.

When we come to interpret the Easter stories in John, we must be clear in our minds that there is a long tradition-history behind them and that John has shaped them to fit his own theology of Easter. Here again, then, what we have is theological narratives with a few bits of historical tradition embedded in them. The truth of these stories is to be found first and foremost in the statements they are endeavoring to make as stories. In his Easter stories John wants to demonstrate the basic assertions Jesus develops so fully in the farewell discourses.

One aspect in particular catches our attention, especially when we take the supplementary chapter 21 into account, namely, the figure of the beloved disciple ("the disciple whom Jesus loved"), who is here pushed into the foreground. The conclusion of chapter 21 will give us an opportunity to discuss this problem in greater detail.

The edition of John's gospel that we now have contains two traditions regarding Easter: the Jerusalem Easter tradition is exclusively followed in chapter 20, while in chapter 21 the Galilean Easter tradition is followed no less exclusively. Even in John the Jerusalem Easter tradition is probably secondary. It is connected with the empty tomb, and since John links not only Mary Magdalene but also the two disciples with this traditional spot, the focus of attention is inevitably on Jerusalem and continues to be until the first conclusion of the gospel (20:30-31). In my opinion the supplementary chapter represents the older Easter tradition when it reports an Easter appearance in Galilee; this is not to say, of course, that other material has not been added to this appearance.

The Discovery of the Empty Tomb
(20:1–10)

In this first pericope two narrative threads are interwoven: first, the discovery of the empty tomb, in this case by Mary Magdalene alone, along with the subsequent meeting of Mary with the risen Jesus (vv. 1, 11-18); second, the "race" of the two disciples—Peter and the "other disciple whom Jesus loved"—to the empty tomb (vv. 3-10). Verse 2 supplies a connection between the two stories. Both stories (perhaps we should more accurately speak of three stories) are originally independent of one another: "Whereas the account of Mary is derived from the tradition to which the synoptic stories about the grave also belong, the story about Peter and the beloved disciple doubtless goes back to the Evangelist."[155] This last is also true in very large measure of verses 11-18. Behind the story of the race there is, of course, the tradition of the Lord appearing first to Peter, but this is elsewhere mentioned only in passing and never handed down as a separate story.

Verse 1 is part of the Mary story and recalls the corresponding accounts in the synoptic gospels (cf. Mark 16:1-8; Matt. 28:1-10; Luke 24:1-11). Here, however, it is Mary alone who comes to the tomb very early "while it was still dark." For what purpose does she come? The reason that brings the women to the tomb, namely to anoint Jesus (cf. Mark 16:1), is missing in John because the body of Jesus has already received this pious service at the original burial. It is probably useless to look for special reasons on Mary's part, since what we have here is in all likelihood only a part of an older tradition. Perhaps in John's mind Mary is motivated by special grief.

The decisive thing is that Mary "sees that the stone has been taken away from the tomb"; this too, of course, is a part of the tradition (cf. Mark 16:3-4 par.). At this point the fragment of tradition ends. We get the impression that in John Mary is seized with terror at the sight of the empty tomb. She does not enter it but immediately runs off to "Simon Peter and the other disciple whom Jesus loved" and tells them, "They have taken my Lord from the tomb, and we do not know where they have laid him." Is the plural "*we* do not know" an echo of the tradition according to which Mary Magdalene did not go alone to the empty tomb on Easter morning but in the company of other women? As the text shows, Mary already has a sure explanation for the fact of the empty tomb: someone has taken the Lord away; later, of course, this will prove to be a misreading of the situation.

It is noticeable that in the Johannine Easter stories the address "Lord" occurs with special frequency as a christological title of majesty.[156] It occurs 14 times, or a good third of all the instances in John. But in the Easter stories the title has a special aura about it; the dominant tone is a peculiar shifting back and forth between intimacy and distance or a kind of solemn embarrassment. From the very outset the risen Jesus is no longer a part of this world; he has taken his abode in the divine sphere, so that the intimate modes of address characteristic of the disciples' earthly dealings with him are in large measure lacking.

The opening of the story introduces a certain tension. The tomb is open; Jesus is presumably no longer there. Mary brings this alarming news to the two disciples—Peter and the beloved disciple—and it causes them to hasten to the tomb in order to find out what is going on. The following account is very detailed; John evidently intends it to mean something special. Peter and the other disciple go to the tomb but not in a leisurely fashion; their going becomes a real race. The two start together but the other disciple runs faster than Peter and reaches the tomb first. Instead of immediately entering it, however, he remains outside, being content for the moment to lean in and see some linen cloths lying there. He then waits for Peter to arrive and enter first.

Peter naturally sees more: not only the linen cloths but the handkerchief which is lying apart. Here again John's special feeling for order is in evidence: the resurrection of Jesus leaves no disorder behind in the empty tomb. Only now that Peter has inspected the tomb does the other disciple enter who—as is emphasized once again—had in fact reached the tomb first. Then comes the remarkable statement, "And he saw and believed. For they did not yet know the scripture, that he had to rise from the dead." Then the disciples return home.

The whole story is quite extraordinary; we can sense something going on in the writer's mind throughout it, but after reading it we are not very sure of just what he means by it. It is clear, to begin with, that there is a rivalry between Peter and the beloved disciple which finds apt expression in their race. It is, of course, a limited kind of rivalry, for although the beloved disciple reaches the tomb first, looks in curiously, and by so doing perhaps already intuits a good deal, nonetheless he gives Peter precedence. This precedence is evidently connected with the fact that even the Johannine tradition knows that the Lord had appeared first to Peter, and it cannot ignore this. The fourth gospel, like the others, does not deny the special position of Peter. Nonetheless the narrator seems to have a greater interest in the other disciple, and there is a clearly perceptible tendency to bring this other disciple into the foreground and give him a significance which is indeed not greater than that of Peter but which is also not less.

The clearest point of all is that when the other disciple finally enters the tomb, he sees what there is to be seen in the empty grave-chamber and believes. When all is said and done, no encounter with the risen Jesus is necessary. This other disciple is in a way the counterpart and antitype of doubting Thomas and therefore is one of those envisaged in the beatitude: "Blessed are they who do not see and yet believe." On the other hand, not a word is said of Peter's reaction. We may well assume that no doubt is being cast on his faith. Neither do the two disciples need an angelic messenger to give them the news of the resurrection.

Verse 9 with its reference to the Scripture is likewise not easy to understand. No specific text is mentioned, although elsewhere when John speaks of Scripture, he is more frequently referring to a particular passage.[157] Here, it seems, he has in mind the testimony of the Scriptures in their entirety; and as a matter of fact the proof from Scripture was probably connected at a very early stage with testimony to the resurrection (cf., e.g., 1 Cor. 15:3-5). What does the verse mean? Have the two disciples still not realized up to this point that Jesus had to rise? Does John mean that only reflection on the Scripture made the Easter faith real to him? Or is he saying here something similar to what we find in Luke where the risen Jesus himself explains the Scriptures to the disciples: "Then he opened their minds to the understanding of the scriptures" (Luke 24:45; cf. 24:26-27)?

In point of fact, the reinterpretation of the Scriptures, that is, the entire Old Testament, from the standpoint of the post-Easter faith in Christ is one of the most significant elements in the theology of the primitive Church. The primitive Christian conviction that the

120

Scripture is fulfilled in the coming of Jesus and especially in his
death and resurrection led to a new christological understanding of
Scripture. It is probably against this background that John's remark
is to be understood.

Does the story of the disciples' race to the empty tomb have a
symbolic meaning? According to R. Bultmann, the point of the story

> rather . . . must lie in the relation of the two disciples to
> one another, who race to the grave, and each in his own
> way achieves precedence of the other. If Peter and the
> beloved disciple are the representatives of Jewish and Gen-
> tile Christianity, the meaning manifestly then is this: the
> first community of believers arises out of Jewish Christi-
> anity, and the Gentile Christians attain to faith only after
> them. But that does not signify any precedence of the for-
> mer over the latter; in fact both stand equally near the Risen
> Jesus, and indeed readiness for faith is even greater with
> the Gentiles than it is with the Jews: the beloved disciple
> ran faster than Peter to the grave![158]

R. Mahoney develops a different interpretation of the passage.[159]
According to him there is no opposition between the two disciples
and consequently no contrast between their personal or symbolic
qualities. The decisive point is rather to be located in the different
actions which each performs and which complement one another:
Peter comes in order, as it were, to determine the facts in an official
way, while the other disciple comes in order to see them and believe.
In this view, it is not the persons as such that are important but
chiefly *their functions.*[160] It is quite possible, and in keeping with
the juridical thinking of the fourth evangelist, that he has Peter and
the beloved disciple represent the two witnesses principle of which
he shows himself aware in other passages (cf. Deut. 19:15: "Only
on the testimony of two or three other witnesses is a final decision
to be rendered in a case").

If we bear in mind an essential defect in the synoptic stories of
the women at the empty tomb, namely that in the Jewish view of
things women were incapable of being witnesses, then it may well
be that John wanted to replace these stories with one better capable
of providing proof. Then Peter and the other disciple become the
necessary two witnesses to the empty tomb, a function which the
women and Mary Magdalene could not exercise by themselves.

Given this context and purpose, the appearance of the angel could likewise be omitted completely, even though the omission introduces a contradiction into the story.

This interpretation does not mean that other purposes do not also come into play. Thus the contrast between the witness who sees and believes without himself meeting the risen Jesus, and Thomas who acts in a way diametrically opposed, is probably intentional. For, in the last analysis, the Easter faith as seen by John can do without the Easter appearances.

The Risen Christ Appears to
Mary Magdalene (20:11–18)

The meeting of Jesus and Mary Magdalene may be implicitly a response to a legend according to which the gardener in charge of the area that contained the tomb removed the body of Jesus.

The account, as presented by John, is a direct answer to the Jewish objections and the doubts they occasioned. In particular, the figure of the gardener and the suspicion that he might have removed the body of Jesus have their origin here. The gardener is a figure vouched for in tradition, and so the question of why Mary Magdalene should have taken him as such is out of place. Later Jewish polemic contains various accounts of how the body of Jesus came to be missing. Far the most frequent form they take is that "Judah the gardener," an honest man, had foreseen the likelihood of the deception and so removed the body.[161]

According to this interpretation John cleverly took the polemical figure of the gardener and reinterpreted it with the help of the confusion motif (v. 15). But even then the polemical purpose is secondary in John; the important thing in the story is the meeting of Jesus and Mary and her recognition of him.

Mary has returned to the tomb (v. 11). By not adverting directly to this circumstance the evangelist shows that he is making an artificial join here. Now Mary stands outside in front of the tomb and weeps; the reason for her sorrow is the complete absence of Jesus, who has not only died but has had his body stolen or mislaid. This is the sorrow of which Jesus had spoken in the farewell discourse: "Truly, truly, I tell you, you will weep and mourn, but the world will rejoice; you will have sorrow,* but your sorrow will be changed to joy" (16:20). This change of sorrow to joy is illustrated in the story of Mary.

The change begins, though very hesitantly, when Mary, weeping, leans into the tomb and looks, and then suddenly sees two angels in white robes sitting there. The gleaming white robes are a symbol of the heavenly world. The figure of the angel is part of the Easter stories from the very beginning (cf. Mark 16:5-7; Matt. 28:2-7; Luke 24:4). In Mark the figure is that of an angelic messenger who has a clearly defined function in the Markan story of Easter: he is the one who gives the women the Easter message as a communique from heaven. For an angel to bring the message of Jesus' resurrection is a way of saying that this is a supernatural event that can be revealed only by heaven and that knowledge of it cannot also be acquired by natural means. According to Mark the angel's message is, "Fear not! You are looking for Jesus the Nazarene who was crucified; he is risen, he is not here! Look at the spot where they laid him!" (Mark 16:6).

Matthew introduces a strongly dramatic element into the scene: to the accompaniment of a great earthquake the messenger from God descends from heaven, rolls the stone from the tomb, and sits on it. He then gives the women the Easter message in terms similar to those in Mark but with a few additions (Matt. 28:2-7). In Luke, too, the angels have their place in the Easter story; but in Luke there are already two angels, as there are in his story of the ascension of Jesus (Luke 24:4; Acts 1:10-11). The raising of the number to two is probably Luke's doing. The two angels again deliver the Easter message.

The most striking thing in John's account is doubtless the fact that while the angels are present as traditional figures they no longer have to deliver the Easter message. According to John the Easter faith comes into existence only through encounter with the risen Jesus himself. What function, then, do the two angels still have? They are sitting within the grave-chamber, at the head and foot of it. Are they there to guard the tomb? This does not make much sense. As John depicts the scene, the impression we get is of a pious

123

picture such as artists have often painted. *The presence of the angels marks the holy place* which functions as a sign for the world of the resurrection of Jesus.

When the angels say to Mary, "Woman, why are you weeping?" they are preparing her for her meeting with Jesus. In response, Mary can only admit her perplexity and helplessness: "They have taken my Lord away" (or: have gotten rid of my Lord) "and I do not know where to find him."

After saying this "Mary turns around" to look behind her. Now she sees Jesus standing there but does not recognize him. At this point it becomes fully clear that John is making extensive use in his Easter stories of a cryptic metaphorical language that points to something deeper. The action of turning around expresses in a sensible way the event that is taking place, namely that the entire situation is now turned around. The failure to recognize Jesus as well as the subsequent confusion of him with the gardener show how alien the *wholly other* is from the normal human situation.

The Easter message and the reality it reflects do not originate in the actualities and hopes of the world. The message conveys not something that people have always known but the eschatologically new. Even the words of Jesus, "Woman, why are you weeping? Whom are you seeking?" do not as yet free Mary from her perplexity. In fact she takes Jesus for the gardener. Her suspicion is that he is the one who has removed the body: "Then tell me where you have laid him, and I will take him." Here again John is indicating how utterly beyond all human imagining the Easter event is.

The recognition scene follows (v. 16). Jesus calls Mary by name. Now comes the real "turning": Mary turns around and says only, "Rabbuni, Teacher." Here John once again shows his astonishing skill at bringing out the essentials of a scene in a few words. It is a scene that invites us to dwell on it, to meditate on it; we are reminded spontaneously of Giotto's famous picture of it. Encounter, recognition, the immense surprise that one had ceased to expect—but each person can think of other aspects of the scene. As John describes the meeting, a very personal relationship of confidence and love that formerly existed is now renewed; more than that, the relationship is now permanent. And it is the risen Jesus himself who renews it by his salutation which is that of both a sovereign and a friend.

If we ask what kind of a world is being conjured up in this story, it is extremely difficult to give an answer. It is a new and different world in which the laws and standards of the world with which we are familiar are evidently no longer valid. The other Easter stories convey the same message; for example, when Jesus suddenly stands in the midst of the disciples, even though they "had made the place tight against outsiders." But, according to John's portrayal of it, this other world is a reality right within the familiar world; he so narrates the incident that we do not in any way get the impression of a fantasy world or a fairy-tale world. In fact, at the climax of the story, which is the meeting of Jesus and Mary, the narrative takes on the tone of tender and immensely attractive human feeling, so that the angels vanish utterly from view. Nothing more is said of them.

The salutation of Jesus, "Mary," and the word with which Mary turns to Jesus, "Rabbuni" (we can imagine this turning only as something sudden and filled with joyous surprise) have the tonality of love poetry. As the lover calls his beloved and she answers him, so do Jesus and Mary meet in John's description. We can understand only too well that Mary should feel a need to lay hold of Jesus. That John thinks the same is evident from verse 17 where Jesus expressly says, *Noli me tangere!* "Do not take hold of me!"

"Taking hold of" or "grasping" is the human way to be sure one is dealing with a reality. "Sense knowledge is for us human beings the criterion of real being. When Aristotle gives primacy to the sense of touch, he has achieved what we must regard as a phenomenological breakthrough of the first order."[162] "Taking hold of" also expresses the entire human process of coming into contact; it can be regarded as a metaphor for the whole range of human contacts. In fact, the word "con-tact" means etymologically a touching of any kind, a communication of a very general kind. Thus "taking hold of" is one of the elementary ways in which the person in the world apprehends external reality. In this context, then, the phrase, "Do not take hold of me," can only mean that the risen Jesus cannot be apprehended in the manner which is proper to the present world. Encounter and contact with the risen Jesus take place on a different level, that is, in faith, through the word, or in the Spirit. It is not possible truly to lay hold of the risen Christ in this world.

The intention of what John is saying becomes even clearer if we compare it with a passage in Luke (24:36-43). There we read,

While they were still speaking of these events, he himself was suddenly standing in their midst. In their anxiety and fear they thought they were seeing a ghost. Then he said to them, "Why are you so troubled? Why do you allow such doubts to arise in your hearts? Look at my hands and feet: it is I myself! *Take hold of me and see; no ghost has flesh and bones as you see I have.*" As he said this, he showed them his hands and feet. They were filled with joy and wonder, but still could not believe it. Then he said to them, *"Do you have anything to eat?" They gave him a piece of baked fish. He took it and ate it before their eyes.*

Luke's orientation is different from John's. In Luke's account Jesus says expressly that they are to take hold of him. There is evidently an apologetic tendency to materialization at work. That is, Luke's intention is to represent the reality of the risen Jesus in as graphic a way as possible with the help of the idea of *materiality*. We are dealing here, of course, with a literary device; Luke does not intend to make any statement about the nature of the resurrection body. More than any other of the evangelists he is meeting the human need of some sensible assurance regarding reality; given the nature of human beings his procedure has its justification. On the other hand, this Lukan approach creates great difficulties in our contemporary situation. John's presentation of the meeting of Jesus with Mary is probably a deliberate reaction against any tendency to materialization in the understanding of Easter, such as we find in Luke.

The problem is that with the human desire to lay hold of there is all too often linked another tendency: the desire to take possession of something, to have it at our disposal, to hold on to it. Now if the risen Jesus cannot and will not be laid hold of, it is clear that he is in no way at our disposal. This realization in turn reflects a basic post-Easter experience in regard to Jesus and the tradition about him, namely that it is impossible for us to reach him by means of any knowledge we may have at our disposal, whether it be historical or systematico-theological. This is not to say that such knowledge has no value; it does make possible many and varied approximations. Possibly one of the most important effects of the Easter faith is to lead us to an ultimate boundary, where we gradually realize that *there is something not at our disposal*, and thus to bring us to an acknowledgment of this something which is utterly beyond our reach.

To say that something is not at our disposal is not to say that it is simply unknowable, much less that it is unreal. As a matter of fact, as is the case with Jesus, we can have rather extensive knowledge of it. But this knowledge no longer provides us with certainties; in fact, it removes plain certainties and provides instead a broad, open space of freedom. The dividing line between faith and unbelief may be determined precisely by whether people acknowledge that which is not at their disposal and allow it to matter for them or whether on the contrary they endeavor by every possible means either to eradicate it or to gain control of it. To try to eliminate or deny that which is not at human disposal is the form the unbelief of the world takes; to try by every means to control it is the form ecclesiastical and theological unbelief takes.

In his Easter stories, John does a better job than the other evangelists of showing the radical impossibility of having Jesus at our disposal. This impossibility, which does not, however, exclude the abiding closeness of Jesus to us in the future, is given sensible manifestation in that Jesus ascends and returns to the Father: "Then Jesus said, 'Do not take hold of me, for I have not yet ascended to the Father. Go to my brothers and tell them: I am ascending to my Father and your Father, to my God and your God.' " The renunciation of a material sensible form of communication does not mean that all communication with Jesus is impossible. In fact, the departure of Jesus to the Father will create the basis for the abiding communion between Jesus and the community of disciples, as the farewell discourses have already indicated in various ways. The present scene reminds us of this.

John here returns once again to the descent-ascent schema he has used so often: Jesus descended from heaven as the incarnate Logos; now that his work is completed he returns again to the Father. Here John is describing what traditional Christian language calls the ascension of Christ, for in John Easter, ascension, and Pentecost form a compact unity. For this reason all three take place on one and the same day in John. The distribution over a longer period model, according to which forty days pass between Easter and the ascension and ten more between the ascension and Pentecost, goes back to

127

Luke. The Church adopted this Lukan model for its liturgical year.

The risen Jesus charges Mary to announce his return to the Father to the disciples, "my brothers." John sees the Easter event itself as the return of Jesus to the Father. The expression "my brothers" is a striking one. Here it connotes the new relationship Jesus now has to his disciples as he expressly includes them in his own relationship to God: "I no longer call you servants but friends" (15:15). For this reason, the expression "to my Father and your Father, to my God and your God" is meant to indicate a sharing, not a reservation: through the resurrection of Jesus the disciples at last participate in his relationship to God. The point, therefore, is not that Jesus is distinguishing between his own metaphysical relationship to God and the relationship of the disciples to God as something secondary, non-metaphysical, and merely moral. Such metaphysical categories are not applicable in the New Testament and only distort the meaning. The sense is rather that for the community of disciples there is no longer any distinction between the God and Father of Jesus and their own God and Father.

The formula is to be understood in the light of similar communication formulas in the Old Testament: "Your people are my people, and your God my God" (Ruth 1:16). The only difference is that in John the formula is reversed. According to his understanding of revelation, people cannot simply choose their God for themselves; instead they are chosen by God, and this through the mediation of Jesus.

The Appearance to the Disciples
(20:19–23)

The Easter appearance of Jesus to the disciples, which according to John takes place on Easter day itself, involves the paradoxical notion of a being that is spiritual and passes through closed doors, and yet has such material qualities that it can be accurately identified. In dealing with this passage it is absolutely necessary to start at the literary level. Questions that used to be raised in connection with it—regarding the subtle character of the risen body of Jesus or the superhuman powers the risen Jesus possesses—are fanciful

128

and mistake the point of the texts, to say nothing of being impossible to answer. The evangelist's problem was that he had to speak of the utterly incomprehensible in a comprehensible, intelligible way. Once we are clear on this point, the story becomes quite reasonable.

In its theological and literary form the story moves with the sureness of a sleepwalker along the outermost edges of what can be conceived and expressed. Moreover, the language John uses is graphic enough to make the symbolic intent of the various images quite clear. Misunderstandings can arise only if the reader misses the symbolism and looks instead for a realistic explanation. The application of depth-psychology research into symbolism is not only permissible in reading such texts as these but fits in perfectly with the character of the texts.

In 16:33b we were told, "In the world you have fear; but take heart, I have overcome the world." The Easter story picks up the theme and shows the fear that has come upon the disciples due to the absence of Jesus: "On the evening of the first day of the week, when the doors were shut where the disciples were. . . ." John gives no details of where in fact the disciples were; the text contains no indication of place. The evangelist's concern is to show the fear of the disciples: they have barred the doors so that no stranger and especially no enemy may enter. The very language of the narrative brings out both the fear and withdrawal of the disciples and the way in which the risen Jesus overcomes these. Simply by reason of this literary symbolism we may conclude that however great the fear and withdrawal may be, the risen Lord has power to make his way through the closed doors. In this way, John illustrates the resurrection and, in a sense, the identity of Jesus and the paraclete as well. The risen Jesus himself is already the other paraclete; he already shows those characteristics of pneumatic reality with power over spirits that marks his new presence in the community of disciples. Thus the risen Jesus comes again and again into a closed world in order by his action to turn it into an open world.

The appearance of the risen Jesus to the disciples is due to the free initiative of the risen Jesus himself. To say this is to say also that on our side there is no possibility of securing ourself against this appearance of Jesus. In the present passage the fear of the disciples is directed at the Jews. Also meant however is the fear and withdrawal of the disciples in relation to a possible appearance of Jesus, in relation to the living reality of Jesus in the present time of the Church and of the world generally. This can be seen in the fact that the question of what is Jesus' will frequently becomes a critical and disturbing question for the Church at moments when it touches in a sensitive way foregone conclusions long since embodied in the status quo.

No matter what the reason for the fear and withdrawal, the untrammeled glorious freedom of the risen Lord, the living Jesus, enables him to be suddenly there in the midst of his disciples and to offer them the Easter greeting of peace, "Peace be with you!" Peace is the supreme gift of the risen Jesus. This peace includes the great universal reconciliation which he effected by his death for the life of the world. The peace of the risen Lord is the peace which the crucified Jesus won by his suffering, that is, which he first made possible by his suffering and death. It is the peace that emerges from the sacrifice of Jesus, from his involvement in the deadliest of all conflicts. The biblical name for this deadliest of conflicts is sin. The word means people's self-isolation, separation, and withdrawal from the ground of their being and from their fellow human beings. Consequently, the Easter victory of Jesus over the world by its nature also includes the ultimate victory in the conflict of conflicts. When the risen Jesus speaks of peace, the word and reality include the reconciliation which he (actively!) brought about by his suffering.

In this context the element of identification is also important to John. The risen Christ is the crucified Jesus, and vice versa; that is why he shows the disciples his hands and side; the wounds of Jesus are identifying marks. The risen and glorified Christ has not simply shed his earthly history and its suffering. Rather, this history has so marked him, once and for all, that the risen Jesus and the crucified Jesus must not be separated from one another. The Easter faith of the Christian is therefore not an illusory exaltation beyond the suffering of the world. What this faith does amid the inexplicable, meaningless suffering of the world is provide a hope that the suffering can be overcome. This indissoluble union of cross and resurrection finds convincing expression in the picture John paints here. Matthias Grünewald has given artistic expression to this same idea in his Isenheim Altar paintings.

Now the fear of the disciples is changed into joy, the basic mood of Easter: "Then the disciples rejoiced when they saw the Lord" (v. 20b).

With this appearance of Jesus John connects the action that establishes the Church, namely, the sending of the disciples by the risen Lord. Jesus repeats his greeting of peace, in order to make it clear that the subsequent sending of the disciples has its ground in the reality of Easter as peace and reconciliation. The purpose of the sending is to pass on to the entire world the peace which Jesus has brought about.

"As the Father has sent me, so I send you" (v. 21b), is John's way of expressing the foundation and mission of the community of Jesus' disciples, the Church. The disciples here represent the entire Church and not a special hierarchic group to which a special power is supposedly communicated. In John's story there is nothing about a hierarchy of offices or of special powers. Mission carries with it authorization and empowerment. In the background the Jewish legal concept of envoy is probably at work: "A person's envoy is like the person himself." That is, the envoy represents the sender, is entirely at the sender's service, and derives authority from this relationship; at the same time, the envoy is to be given the honor due to the sender.

According to John, Jesus is par excellence the envoy and revealer of God. When he here delegates his own mission, the sense is that the community of disciples takes over the mission and therefore the authority of Jesus. But no one can validly represent Jesus who does not at the same time accept the way of Jesus, his basic attitude of reconciliation, and his renunciation of power and domination that is evidenced in the washing of the feet and subsequently throughout the passion narrative. If we follow John, it is not possible to interpret mission as a formal canonical transmission of the power attaching to an ecclesiastical office; to do so would be to limit John's thought in an arbitrary and unwarrantable manner. On the contrary, Christian authority has always been subject to an objective criterion, for its must always answer to the claims put forth by the example of Jesus in the washing of the feet and thus by the service given by Jesus. And this service is a service of love, peace, and reconciliation.

Along with the mission comes the bestowal of the Spirit as the source of the ability to carry it out: "After speaking these words he breathed on them and said to them, 'Receive the Holy Spirit' " (v.

131

22). The risen Jesus communicates the Holy Spirit to the community of his disciples. Here again symbolism plays a part. The "breathing on" recalls Genesis 2:7: "Then the LORD God formed man from the dust of the earth and breathed into his nostrils the breath of life, and man became a living being." The communication of the Spirit is a communication of new life. John here sums up in a simple image the theme that has occupied his gospel from beginning to end: Jesus is the giver of eschatological life to humanity. The power here bestowed is meant for the communication of life.

This communication of life is here described by means of the traditional Christian concept of forgiveness of sins: "Whose sins you forgive, they are forgiven them; whose sins you leave unchanged, they are left unchanged" (v. 23). Forgiveness of sins is a rather esoteric concept today, and to many people no longer says anthing. Originally the reference was to the great purification of one's life, the new start, the new chance in which the past was definitively left behind and no longer had to be taken into account and compensated for. But this change was not effected in any magical way; rather it came about because the community of disciples now accepted the reconciliation which Jesus had won by his suffering, and made it the foundation of their entire action and witness and life.

The alternative "forgive/leave unchanged" recalls the Matthean formulation of the power of the keys as one of "binding and loosing" (Matt. 18:18; 16:19). This alternatives formula already reflects sociological conditions having to do with the practice of the community. The Christian community has already begun, at a rather early date, to formulate conditions for the inclusion and exclusion of members and had appealed to the authority of Jesus for justification in doing so. And yet there is a perceptible tension between Jesus' universal offer of reconciliation and the practice of the Church. There is here a sociological problem, a development that must be measured against the original intention of Jesus.

As all admit, the intention of Jesus is a general divine amnesty, a universal offer of reconciliation and life. The Church, for its part, is to some extent captive to the world's way of doing things, and consequently is not absolutely free of group interests and desires for domination. It must therefore be repeatedly confronted in a critical way with the original intention of Jesus. The danger of the transmission of alternative powers to "forgive/leave unchanged" or "bind and loose" is that, as has frequently happened in the course of history, the official Church may succumb to the illusion that it can dispose of reconciliation at its own discretion.

The authority to forgive sin is promised, then, to the entire Church, so that all members of the Church participate in it. John sees the forgiveness of sins as an essential aspect of the Easter reality, as the new start. His Easter messeage is that through Jesus God has effected the great reconciliation, the great peace in the world; this peace must be proclaimed and offered to the entire world as the new chance at life. That is why the community of disciples exists.

The universality of this offer of grace is contradicted when hierarchic powers are deduced from it, certain sins are reserved, a trade in indulgences, even a spiritual trade, is instituted, and so on. Nor is anything said in the text about the outward forms the forgiveness of sins is to take. Such forms have no absolute or timeless significance. They have changed frequently in the course of history and will change again in the future. The greatest danger has always been that official regulation of the practice of penance has manipulated and limited the universal offer of peace in an intolerable manner. In large measure, the offer of peace has been turned into a means of intraecclesial social control.

At bottom, every believer who knows that the power of the new eschatological life has laid hold of him has the power to forgive sins in everyday life and in regard to every human being. The organized official forgiveness of sins, on the other hand, derives its justification in part from the needs and structures of the community, and in part also from the fact that the community as a whole must give the witness of the forgiveness of sins to the world. This witness, however, is never given in some ahistorical context but always in specific, concrete historical circumstances and must take into account social conditions in the environing world. It is always a dangerous situation, however, when conditions in the environing world obscure and repress the witness of free and unconditional reconciliation and thereby the intention of Jesus as well. This is the case when, for example, the official Church operates with privileges and special graces for which there is no theological ground. Or when a wrong stress leads to excessive emphasis on pious works, as happened in the pre-Reformation period, and thus radically distorts the fundamental attitude expressed in penance.

It is important today again that the unlimited offer of reconciliation be given new and convincing expression in our modern situation. The new forms of penitential service have in large measure represented a certain progress insofar as they supplement the tradition of individual confession. The social aspect of reconciliation is now more clearly seen than it used to be. Nor is there any objection to be raised in principle against the dismantling of a privileged power to reconcile. We must even regard it as a very positive step when base communities of Christians again make use of possibilities long withheld from them and even utterly disallowed them by Church law. The important thing is that Christian groups and perhaps someday the universal Church and its authorities should make reconciliation through Christ real in the eyes of society and turn it into something credible and convincing.

Blessed Are They Who Do Not See and Yet Believe: Doubting Thomas (20:24–29)

This passage is not primarily concerned with "unbelieving Thomas," who as such has become a stock figure, but with the immediate addressees of the gospel of John, that is, with those Christians who had no direct contact with the earthly Jesus or even with the first disciples and apostles, and to whom the risen Lord has not appeared. In a wider sense, the addressees include all the Christians of later generations, for their situation is the same. The beatitude at the end, which sums up the point of the story, is meant for all of them: "Blessed are they do not see and yet believe."

In the very first part of his Easter story John has already made it clear that, in his view, Easter faith in the living Lord Jesus Christ does not depend unconditionally on the Easter appearances. The beloved disciple needed only to look into the empty tomb, and he believed: "He saw and believed." It is possible that, as far as their relation to faith is concerned, John passed the same judgment on the Easter appearances that he did on miracles: "If you do not see

signs and wonders, you do not believe" (4:48b). For him the signs
and wonders are primarily a concession to human weakness. They
can even become dangerous for those who see only the sensational
results of the miracles and do not grasp the symbolism by means
of which they are meant to bring people finally to faith in Jesus. In
the last analysis, however, people come to faith only through the
word of proclamation about Jesus. This principle holds even with
regard to Easter faith: when all is said and done, it is not dependent
on the appearances.

It really ought not to surprise us that there should be any room
for talk of doubt in the circle of those who believed in the resurrection of Jesus. The real surprise, on the contrary, would be that
no doubts arose at all. The evangelists speak in various ways of doubt
with regard to the Easter faith. Thus Matthew says, "And when
they saw him, they prostrated themselves before him. But some
doubted" (Matt. 28:17). And Luke notes the attitude of the disciples
when they heard the women's story: "But they regarded their words
as idle gossip and did not believe them" (Luke 24:10). In the address
of Paul on the Areopagus (Acts 17:22-34) the Easter faith becomes
the critical point for the hearers and finally causes them to reject
the Christian preaching: "When they heard Paul talk of 'resurrection
from the dead,' some jeered and the others said, 'We shall listen
to you on this point some other time' " (Acts 17:32).

Even though historical literalness cannot be claimed for these
various remarks, we must surely accept the fact that in primitive
Christianity there were doubts about the Easter faith from the very
beginning. There is positive evidence of this in the great chapter
(15) on the resurrection in the First Letter to the Corinthians, where
Paul, though not dealing directly with doubts about the Easter faith,
is nonetheless forced to counter radical misunderstandings of it. As
a matter of fact, this doubt has been a recurring phenomenon
throughout the entire history of Christianity, whether it has had to
do with the idea of resurrection as such or specifically with the
resurrection of Jesus or whether the point has been the inconsistencies of the reports about Easter.

In this context the problem of doubt needs to be handled with
an awareness of its special character. For, after all, when judged by
general human experience, faith in a resurrection from the dead is
a paradox that directly rouses opposition and necessarily runs up

against prejudgments and misunderstandings. Such prejudgments and misunderstandings can hardly be disparaged as doubts, much less as doubts against faith. If a person wants to understand and accept, in its authentic religious sense, the symbolic language of resurrection from the dead and of the resurrection of Jesus, it will be repeatedly necessary to articulate the misunderstandings and prejudgments in order to see through them and come to grips with them.

If *death* is the strongest negation we know of human life and life's meaning, then the Easter faith is the strongest "No" ever directed to this negation, and an unconditional "Yes" to the positive meaning of life. Christian faith sees this "Yes" as grounded in God and the risen Jesus: "But God is faithful so that our word to you is not both 'Yes' and 'No.' For the Son of God, Christ Jesus, whom we—I myself and Silvanus and Timothy—preached to you, is not both 'Yes' and 'No,' but in him the 'Yes' has come. For, however many the promises of God are, in him they have received their 'Yes.' Therefore it is also through him that we give our 'Amen' for the glory of God" (2 Cor. 1:18-20). Seen from this point of view, the Easter faith does not involve simply the particular problem of whether or not the resurrection of Jesus took place, but the entire person of Jesus and whether and to what extent he comes before us convincingly in his role as revealer of God.

The idea of God is also involved here, at least from the New Testament standpoint. For in this context God is not thought of in an abstract way as the immutable, self-contained, eternal being, but as the active, mighty God who is infinitely concerned about the salvation of human beings. Jesus of Nazareth is the witness to the God who loves humanity. To this extent the Easter faith is in fact central to the Christian understanding of faith, and this because the person of Jesus himself, with his here-and-now claims on us, is central to a Christian understanding of faith. Let us repeat: the important thing here is not a dogmatic formula but the living, Spirit-filled meaning to which the formula refers. The important thing is the living Spirit of Jesus of Nazareth in our present lives.

When viewed in this perspective, even doubt regarding the Easter faith can be a first step in approaching the meaning of this faith. For many it is probably a necessary step, since the ecclesiastical interpretation of Easter has become formalistic and therefore distorts the true meaning of the Easter faith more often than it sheds light. It is precisely doubt that in many instances leads to a thoroughgoing discussion of the reality that is doubted; the doubt brings us closer to the reality and deeper into it. If Easter is connected with the experience of what is not at our disposal, as we said earlier, then, even though the doubt is motivated by a desire for a more secure proof and foothold, it is overcome by an opposite process, insofar as the person learns to renounce any evidentiary proof and solid foothold and to surrender to the faith to which Jesus of Nazareth bears witness. This is the way along which Thomas is led in this story.

Thomas, called "the twin," appears several times in the gospel of John (cf. 11:16b; 14:5; 21:2). His name is known from the tradition.[163] It is not possible now to say for sure why the fourth evangelist is particularly interested in him. Perhaps the evangelist had some special traditions at hand; but perhaps, too, we are already at the beginning of the legend about Thomas. In any event, the legend is of no importance for our present story, since what the story has to say is contained entirely within the passage itself. Thomas is of interest here not as a historical figure but as the type of a certain kind of behavior that is described in the course of the story. Here he is the antagonist who doubts the resurrection of Jesus but is finally won over through an encounter with the risen Christ, and confesses his faith in the living Lord Jesus.

Thomas is introduced with the explanation that he had not been present at the first appearance to the disciples. He himself had not experienced the real thing but was dependent on news from others, namely, the other disciples. This fact situates him as a type: he was not an eyewitness but received the Easter message from others. His situation is typical inasmuch as it has been the situation in which preaching has operated since the days of the apostles.

The disciples tell Thomas, "We have seen the Lord!" In response, Thomas demands a direct experience of his own if he is to believe in the resurrection of Jesus. In fact, this direct experience must be of the most solid kind: he must "see" and "lay hold of": "Unless I see the mark of the nails in his hands and put my finger in the mark of the nails and lay my hand on the wound in his side, I will not believe" (v. 25). Thomas insists on verification, and indeed on concrete sensible verification which, as John tells the story, resembles an experimental proof in the natural sciences.

Here we may ask whether this story and its details have not played a decisive part in the development of modern consciousness. We have in the story the doubt that later developed into methodical doubt (Descartes); we also have the desire for empirical confirmation. Doesn't this Thomas look like the first Cartesian before Descartes, that is, like a real modern man? He exemplifies a particular basic outlook and a particular understanding of reality. He is bent on receiving an assurance about the risen Jesus that is based on evidence and requires that Jesus put himself at his disposal.

The sequel of the story is not precisely what careless interpreters often represent it as being. For, if we look closely, Thomas does not get the kind of palpable assurance he had wanted.

A week later the disciples are gathered again, and this time Thomas is with them (v. 26). The first thing that strikes us is the regularity: the first day of the week, or Sunday, has already become the fixed day on which the Christian community assembles; on this day the liturgy is celebrated. The evangelist is here reading the current practice of his day back into the very earliest period after Easter. In addition, John's telling of the story allows us to infer that, in his view, the presence of the risen Jesus can be experienced in the community's liturgy.

The same thing happens here as at the first Easter appearance: Jesus again enters though the doors are closed, and he says, "Peace be with you!" Perhaps the greeting of peace was the usual greeting among the Christians of the Johannine communities, and the liturgy may have opened with it (cf. the corresponding greeting in today's liturgy, "The Lord be with you!"). Then the risen Jesus invites Thomas, "Put your finger here and see my hands; put out your hand and place it on my side, and be no longer unbelieving but believing" (v. 27).

We have here a not uncommon literary motif: the doubter who has talked big and expressed a wish or request he was really not convinced could be fulfilled is taken at his word.[164] John uses the device to describe a situation of radical decision: Thomas is forced to do what he had said he would do. The reader too is shown in an impressive way that the risen Jesus could at any time provide a

138

realistic proof if he wanted to or if he were impudently challenged to do so.

A further element in the structure of the story is that Thomas does not carry out his own stipulation; it is quite enough that he, like the other disciples, should see Jesus. He does not go so far as actually to lay hold of Jesus. Consequently, Thomas really does not experience anything more than do the other disciples. It is enough that he be put on the spot. The evangelist rightly renounces any detailed description of the fulfillment of Thomas' wish. There is no need of it. Correspondingly, Jesus' challenge to Thomas is not that Thomas should now lay hold of him, but rather takes the form of an exhortation: "Be no longer unbelieving but believing." What Jesus asks for is not touch but faith. In this respect the story is consistent with the first story of an Easter appearance, the one to Mary Magdalene. Faith renounces touching or laying hold of, for it, faith, is the acceptance of the impossibility of having the risen Jesus at our disposal. Thomas' response, therefore, is to believe and make a profession of faith, "My Lord and my God!"

This profession of faith is carefully and deliberately placed at the (first) conclusion of John's gospel and therefore at the end of the way along which he had wanted to lead his hearers and readers. Encounter with the risen One makes it fully clear who this Jesus really is. For this reason the confessional formula at this point in John's gospel includes the two highest titles of dignity that there can be for Jesus in the New Testament, namely, the titles of God and Kyrios or Lord.

Both titles are to be read against the background of the entire gospel, in which Jesus is revealer of God and giver of eternal life and stands wholly on the side of God. Even here, however, Jesus is not simply identical with God. At the same time, the essential likeness of Jesus to God is formulated, just as it had already been formulated in the prologue: "In the beginning was the Word, and the Word was with God, and the Word was God" (1:1). Both statements—the one about the divinity of the Word and the one about the divinity of the risen Jesus—must be seen in their reciprocal relationship (cf. also 17:5). The risen Jesus has entered that divine glory from which he had earlier come forth. He is the exalted Christ who is haloed by the divine nimbus. The fact that the vanquished doubter utters the highest form of confession of Christ has a special

139

impact, adds a final enhancement. The unsurpassable high point has now been reached.

The gospel of John ends suitably with a beatitude addressed to believers: "Jesus says to him, 'Because you have seen me, you have believed. Blessed are they who do not see and yet believe' " (v. 29).

First Concluding Remark (20:30–31)

As this remark shows, the gospel of John ended here at one time. The author once again summarizes the point of his book about Jesus. First, he indicates its limitations: "There were many other signs that Jesus did in the presence of his disciples which are not written down in this book" (v. 30). Here he gives the reader the impression of a voluminous tradition about Jesus which he has not been able to exhaust. The gospel reports only a small selection of signs (miracle stories).

It is no longer possible to judge, of course, to what extent the author did have other material which he did not use. If we compare John with the synoptic gospels and especially the gospel of Mark, the gospel of John has fewer miracle stories than Mark. And yet, taken as a whole, the tradition regarding Jesus' miracles cannot have been excessively large or contained much more than we have in the testimonies that have come down to us. Additional miracle stories are indeed to be found in the apocryphal gospels of the second century, but these new stories focus on the miracles primarily as sensational, magical occurrences. Their purpose is different than the accounts of miracles in the synoptic gospels and John; the theme of faith plays practically no role in them. John, who stands between the synoptic evangelists and the writers of the apocrypha, has a primarily theological purpose in speaking of signs. He is not concerned simply with the miraculous as such.

This theological purpose is expressed once again: "But these have been written down so that you may believe that Jesus is the Messiah, the Son of God, and that through faith you may have life in his name" (v. 31). This statement holds for the gospel in its entirety, for the latter is intended as a witness to faith. This book is meant to lead the reader to faith in Jesus; specifically, the reader is to acknowledge Jesus as the Messiah, the Son of God, and thus obtain a share in eschatological salvation. This verse is in fact the most concise summary of Johannine theology; if we wanted to give a full explanation of the scope of each concept in this concluding remark, we would have to range back over the entire gospel. Readers who have allowed themselves to be led along to this point know what is being said in this concluding remark.

Supplementary Chapter:
The Appearance of the Risen Jesus
at the Sea of Gennesaret (21:1–25)

This section is found in all the manuscripts that have come down to us; consequently, from the very beginning it belonged to the gospel of John in the published form in which the gospel is known. This supplementary chapter must have been added to the gospel at a very early stage, even before its general diffusion. For there is no doubt that 20:30-31 forms the original conclusion. We expect nothing more. The second ending (21:25) is of a different kind. It does not summarize the content of the gospel as the first conclusion does, but instead makes a rather vague rhetorical flourish when it says that there would not be room enough in the world for all the books needed if one were to write down all that Jesus did. This is evidently only a poor imitation of the first ending.

The supplementary chapter raises a whole series of questions connected chiefly with the origin and authorship of the gospel of John. Who composed and added this supplementary chapter: the evangelist himself or someone else? Is the evangelist to be identified with the beloved disciple? Is the beloved disciple to be identified as someone named John, and if so, who was this John: one of the twelve apostles (the son of Zebedee) or someone else of whom we know nothing more?[165]

To get our bearings here, we must carefully distinguish two questions which are relatively independent of each other. First, there is the literary problem connected with the question of authorship: Do the supplementary chapter and the gospel come from the same author (whoever this author may have been)? Second, there is the problem of the beloved disciple. The main point to be made is that the solution of the first problem is of very little help for the solution of the second. The second problem must be examined as an independent one. Consequently, when the two problems are treated together, very divergent viewpoints are possible.

As regards the first problem—Do the supplementary chapter and the gospel have the same author?—it must be said that a large number of contemporary exegetes think the supplementary chapter does not come from the author (or editor) of the gospel (i.e., chapters 1-20). A chief objection to the same authorship is that if the author were the same, he would in all probability have changed the first ending. Then too there is the great difference with regard to the location of the Easter appearances: Jerusalem in chapter 20, Galilee in chapter 21. Furthermore, the author of chapter 21 writes in a very detached way of the persons and events which have already come up in the gospel. It seems to follow from this that while the author of the supplementary chapter knows the entire gospel of John, he has a very impersonal relationship to it. There are, then, a series of arguments for maintaining that the evangelist who wrote chapters 1-20, and the author of the supplementary chapter are two different persons.[166] We shall say something later about the second problem.

The division of chapter 21 is rather clear. The chapter contains three sections: (a) the Easter appearance (vv. 1-14); (b) Simon Peter (vv. 15-19); (c) the beloved disciple (vv. 20-24) and the second concluding remark (v. 25).

In the first two sections traditions of varying origin are evidently being used. "This new section has for its object the calling of the two disciples, Peter and John."[167] This remark of Schlatter's rightly observes that this chapter offers reflections chiefly on the relationship of Peter and the beloved disciple. The fact of these reflections, which evidently presuppose the death of both disciples and are based on information regarding it, shows that with this text we are in a relatively late period of primitive Christianity, when people were already reflecting on apostolic tradition and its requirements. It is a time when people are beginning to seek legitimacy for their own tradition by tracing it back to a well-known or not so well-known personality; in the process material was often attributed falsely to a famous author (see also the Deutero-Pauline Letters, the Pastoral Letters, 1 and 2 Peter). From this point of view the supplementary chapter is saying something about the question of authorship or, more accurately, about the stand the author of chapter 21 was taking on the problem.

THE EASTER APPEARANCE IN GALILEE (21:1-14)

The supplementary chapter first reports a further Easter appearance, this time in Galilee: "After this Jesus revealed himself again to his disciples by the Sea of Tiberias. Now this is how he revealed himself . . . " (v. 1). To this "again" corresponds the closing remark that this "was the third time Jesus revealed himself to the disciples" (v. 14). These two remarks, which act as a framework, are due to the author of the supplementary chapter who has adapted his text to the text of the gospel which he had before him. He has managed to effect only a superficial adaptation; the internal contradictions are hardly relieved at all.

This is true especially of the Easter appearance itself which, according to his account, takes place in Galilee by the sea, whereas chapter 20 locates all the appearances in Jerusalem. This is of all the greater consequence if 21:1-14 represents in fact an older tradition of Easter accounts that had been deliberately set aside or suppressed. No further attempt is made to render the stay of the disciples intelligible; the gospel of John says nothing of a flight of the disciples such as Mark relates. That this flight is simply presupposed here as a known fact is an indication of an older tradition which is close to that of Mark and Matthew. It is impossible now to determine how such a tradition became available in the milieu of the fourth evangelist; unless of course the hypothesis is correct that in chapter 20 the evangelist has deliberately left aside other traditions which were known to him.

A series of other traditions and motifs has become linked with this special Easter tradition. First, there is the tradition about the great catch of fish (cf. Luke 5:1-11); then there is the call of the first disciples (cf. Mark 1:16-20).[168] In all probability the oldest tradition for the latter story takes the form of a vocation story, such as we find in its simplest form in Mark 1:16-20. This latter passage tells how Jesus calls the brothers Simon (Peter) and Andrew and the two sons of Zebedee to follow him with the words, "Come, follow me!

143

I will make you fishers of men" (Mark 1:17). Out of the image "fishers of men" the tradition of the great catch of fish may have developed, for in Luke the story of the catch closes with the words, "And Jesus said to Simon, 'Fear not! From now on you will catch men' " (Luke 5:10). Contacts between the Johannine and Lukan traditions are to be found in other passages as well, and therefore it may have been by this path that the vocation story became known to the circle which followed the Johannine tradition. In all likelihood, then, the connection of the vocation story with the Easter appearance is secondary.[169]

A further motif is the pairing of bread and fish (v.9), which recalls the miraculous multiplication of loaves.[170] Possibly, too, there is at work the motif of the Easter appearance during a meal (cf. also Luke 24:41). The author has linked these fragments of tradition, which have very diverse origins, and then filled them out with motifs from the Johannine tradition.

The story is introduced as an Easter appearance account, and specifically as an account from the tradition of Easter appearances in Galilee. Verse 2 lists a whole group of disciples. The names of some of them are known from the gospel of John: Simon Peter, Thomas the twin, and Nathanael of Cana (cf. 1:45-50); to these are added the two sons of Zebedee, who do not appear elsewhere in the gospel of John, and two other unnamed disciples.

The account not only clearly supposes the flight of the disciples to Galilee after Good Friday; it also takes it for granted that after Good Friday the disciples return to their old trade as fishermen. For that is probably what lies behind Peter's announcement, "I am going fishing." The other disciples go with him. The motif of lack of success (cf. Luke 5:5) prepares for the great catch of fish. In the early morning Jesus is standing on the shore, but he is not immediately recognized. In this respect the Easter account here resembles the story of the disciples at Emmaus (Luke 24:25-26) with its motif of encounter with a stranger.

In verse 5 a question from Jesus introduces the great catch of fish: "Children, have you anything to eat?" When the disciples answer in the negative, Jesus bids them cast the net on the right side of the boat; there may be a symbolism here which is no longer quite clear to us. The disciples obey and make a very large catch, so that they can barely drag the net to shore. This is a sign that enables the beloved disciple to recognize Jesus: "It is the Lord!" (cf. 20:8). And as in the story told in 20:1-10, so here again the rivalry motif appears, inasmuch as Peter immediately springs into action. He pulls on his outer garment, which he had taken off while fishing, and plunges into the water in order to reach Jesus as quickly as possible. We should not credit the story with any ambition to be realistic and correct, for how was Peter to swim wearing a long outer garment? Or was the water so shallow that he could wade through it? This is probably why verse 8 observes that the boat was not far from shore. The nets are now drawn in to shore.

Verse 9 records a further surprise: On the shore, near Jesus, a coal-fire is burning, and laid on it are a fish and some bread. Is there a symbolism intended here again, perhaps a reference to the Lord's supper? Or is the point rather to correct or clarify the question asked in verse 5, to the effect that the risen One really does not need help from the disciples, nor does he need food, whereas the disciples do? In this second interpretation, the emphasis is on the initiative of Jesus; as in the miraculous multiplication of loaves (6:1-15) Jesus is host to his disciples. Even in the period after Easter, the disciples continue to be dependent on the word of Jesus. That is why we have Jesus ordering the disciples to bring some of the fish they have caught.

Peter, as leader of the disciples, draws the net to shore; it is packed with "one hundred and fifty-three large fish." the number 153 is meant to indicate an extraordinary profusion; the allusion is probably to an extraordinarily successful mission. It is no longer possible to determine whether the number has some further mysterious symbolic meaning.[171] Part of the miracle is that the net is not torn; this may be an allusion to the unity of the Church.

Jesus the host invites the disciples, "Come and eat." Emphasis is placed on the nervousness of the disciples in the presence of this stranger who is nonetheless familiar to them. This aspect probably played a role in the appearance story which serves as the basis of our story here. It brings out the difference between the earthly and the risen Jesus. The latter belongs to the divine world and therefore awakens the awe which is the proper response to the numinous. The statement, "For they knew it was the Lord," alludes to this awe, and once again expresses the fact that the risen One belongs to the realm of God. At the meal itself Jesus continues to play the

145

host: "Jesus comes, takes bread and gives it to them, and the same with the fish" (cf. 6:11). The Easter story ends with the meal.

The author is evidently familiar with the content and theological views of the fourth gospel; from it he has taken some elements that are important for his third Easter story. The following motifs especially are taken from the Johannine tradition: the rivalry motif involving Peter and the beloved disciple (Peter and the two sons of Zebedee must have already been part of the older version of the story), and the emphasis on the role of Jesus as host. The other motifs also have a theological significance. The miraculous catch of fish, along with the net that does not tear, probably symbolizes the mission and therefore the establishment of the Church. The meal motif, on the other hand, points to the Eucharist or, to put it in broader terms, to the regular meal of the community, at which the disciples on each occasion experience once again the presence of the risen Jesus.

The specific reason why the author took up and passed on this story seems to be that it gave him a good opportunity for raising once again the question of Peter and the beloved disciple. For it looks very much as though the beloved disciple were not in the original story. Consequently, he is not to be identified with any of the disciples named. This Easter story is meant primarily as a peg on which to hang the following two sections.

SIMON PETER (21:15–19)

The second section is concerned especially with Simon Peter. Verses 15-17 report three questions of Jesus to Simon Peter, and Peter's three answers; each answer is followed by a commission from Jesus. Verses 18-19 give a brief account of Peter's later destiny.

As in the other gospels and the letters of Paul, so in the gospel of John the figure of Peter plays a very prominent role.[172] In John, as elsewhere, we must distinguish between the historical Peter and the symbolic or typological Peter; the statements made about Simon Peter already suppose his great importance in the primitive Church and therefore are not automatically to be taken as historical reports about Peter. The letters of Paul (Galatians; 1 Corinthians) doubtless

146

bring us closest to the historical Peter; next in historical value are a number of notices in the synoptic gospels and in the Acts of the Apostles. The Johannine tradition regarding Peter is relatively late, and we should be rather skeptical of its accuracy as a picture of the historical Peter. This does not mean, however, that the Johannine tradition may not also include much reliable information.

How does the gospel of John view Peter? Mentions of Peter in John are rather infrequent as compared with those in the synoptic tradition. Lacking, above all, are passages in which Peter is almost stereotyped as spokesman for the disciples. Again, the linking of Peter, James, and John does not occur at all in John. On the other hand, when Peter is mentioned, it is in significant contexts. Thus, according to 1:40-42 Simon Peter is one of the original disciples who had been followers of the Baptist but joined Jesus because of what the Baptist said about him. In 1:33-39 two disciples of the Baptist hear their master's laudatory testimony to Jesus, "Behold the Lamb of God!" and as a result attach themselves to Jesus.

The name of one of the two disciples is not given, but the other is Andrew, brother of Simon Peter (1:40). Andrew meets his brother and leads him to Jesus, telling him, "We have found the Messiah!" Jesus "looks at him and says, 'You are Simon, son of John? Your name will be Cephas' which in translation means 'Rock' [Greek: *petros*]" (1:42). According to this passage, then, "Simon, son of John" (or: "Simon, son of Jonah," according to Matt. 16:17), who, as we are told in 1:44, came from Bethsaida, a place on the north shore of the Sea of Gennesaret, receives the symbolic name of Cephas-Rock (Peter) at his first meeting with Jesus. But John's account of the calling of the disciples contains fictitious elements and cannot be accepted with reservation as historical. Contemporary scholars are not in agreement on whether Peter was surnamed "Rock" by the historical Jesus or whether, on the contrary, the name was given to him only later by the post-Easter community (cf. Matt. 16:17-18). In any case, all the gospels attribute the name-giving to Jesus himself, and this may be historically correct (cf. also Mark 3:16: "He gave Simon the surname Peter"; Luke 6:14).

The symbolic name Rock/Peter soon became a fixed part of Simon's proper name and even replaced the "Simon." The name is not meant as a description of Peter's character but as a sign of his theological role within the group of disciples. According to the testimony of the New Testament, he did not take this role on his own initiative; it was given to him by Jesus. We indicated above the most important aspects of Peter's role after Easter in assembling the community of disciples. His special position is accepted without question in the New Testament texts; similarly, no one in the primitive Church, including Paul, challenged it. In this respect, the gospel of John is no exception.

In 6:66-71 John reports a confession of Peter that has a great deal in common with the corresponding confession in the synoptic gospels (Mark 8:27-30 par. Matt. 16:13-20; Luke 9:18-21). After the great discourse on the bread (6:22-65) many disciples abandoned Jesus, and Jesus asks the Twelve, "Do you also want to go away?" Simon Peter speaks for the rest of the disciples when he answers, "Lord, to whom shall we go? You have words of eternal life. And we have believed and known that you are the Holy One of God" (6:68-69). Peter's confession of Jesus at this historic moment is not questioned by John; "this is an indication of the firm tradition which the fourth evangelist accepts as binding on him, and an important testimonial to the truth of his portrait of Peter."[173]

Peter next comes on the scene only at the washing of the feet, when he first refuses to let Jesus perform this service for him, and then impetuously demands that the Lord wash his head as well (13:6-10). In this scene Peter doubtless serves as a type, since he illustrates a misunderstanding and its resolution. In 13:24-25 Peter, through the agency of the beloved disciple, asks the identity of the betrayer; in 13:36-38 Jesus predicts Peter's denial; according to 18:10-11, Peter cuts off the right ear of Malchus, a servant of the high priest; 18:15-18, 25-27, describes the denial of Peter; and 20:1-10 tells of how Peter and the beloved disciple went to the empty tomb.

The question of the relation between Peter and the beloved disciple arises first in 13:24-25 where Peter inquires about the betrayer. Here the beloved disciple acts as go-between for Jesus and Peter. It is not clear why Peter does not put the question himself. One reason, however, may be that the evangelist wants to make clear at this early point the greater closeness of the beloved disciple to Jesus; this disciple is reclining on the bosom of Jesus. In the race of the disciples to the empty tomb the witness motif is dominant, but the rivalry motif cannot be wholly excluded. The beloved dis-

148

ciple seems to have a greater readiness to believe, but despite this the gospel of John does not play down the importance of Peter. In John the rivalry does not focus on the person of Peter and his role as leader, but has to do rather with greater closeness to Jesus.

"Feed my sheep" (vv. 15-17). Directly after the meal Jesus turns to Simon Peter and addresses him in an especially solemn manner. The solemnity is underscored by the use of the full name "Simon, son of John" three times in a row; this gives the whole proceedings an official character. The ritual is each time the same: (a) address and question; (b) response of Simon Peter; (c) commission to Simon Peter.

The threefold question of Jesus is, "Simon, son of John, do you love me (more than these)?" Peter is being asked about his personal, unreserved commitment to Jesus. Since the name Cephas/Peter is not explicitly mentioned in this context, we may surmise that in the Johannine tradition the symbolic name "Rock" was taken as referring to a wholly special love of Jesus, and specifically an ultimate and unshakeable commitment to him. Such a total and firm love of Jesus seems at the same time to be the inherent prerequisite for the subsequent commission.

Peter twice answers, "Yes, Lord, you know that I love you." Only when the question is again repeated are we told, "Then Peter was saddened that he should ask him a third time, 'Do you love me?' and he says to him, 'Lord, you know everything. You know that I love you'" (v. 17b). The traditional interpretation, which sees in the three questions an allusion to Peter's triple denial, is probably correct. For the fact that Peter was saddened is probably best explained by his recollection of his denial. Consequently, he is ready to love Jesus and commit himself to him without reservation. The Johannine tradition thus lays special emphasis on the idea that Peter's role as "rock" has its basis in his relationship to Jesus and in nothing else. In this John differs from Matthew, in whose gospel the symbol of the rock is immediately given an ecclesiological interpretation: "You are the Rock and on this rock I will build my Church" (Matt. 16:18). In John the christological aspect is more clearly central.

Peter's threefold answer is followed by a threefold commission from Jesus: "Feed my lambs" or "my sheep." In the language of the image this means that Jesus is appointing Peter to be shepherd of

149

his sheep during the time of his absence. The language and therefore the meaning of the statement can be best explained by reference to the discourse on the shepherds (10:14-16) where Jesus describes himself as the good shepherd and speaks of "my sheep". The image of the shepherd had an extensive tradition behind it in the Old Testament and the ancient East and points to Jesus as being the messianic guide to salvation who defends his own to the point of dying for them and thereby establishes the flock which is the messianic community of salvation. He knows his own and he lays down his life for the sheep; he brings together all the sheep of the world, and they shall become one flock, one shepherd.

Here again it is the relationship of believers to Jesus that establishes the flock. According to John, Church always has a christological basis and is never a merely sociological or pure institutional phenomenon. How intimate the relationship is to be regarded is shown in the sentence, "I know mine, and mine know me, just as the Father knows me and I know the Father" (10:14b-15a). The relationship is thus unique, being based on the relationship between Jesus and his Father. Consequently, this relationship that sustains and constitutes Jesus' community of salvation is absolutely nontransferable. Consequently, too, we must be careful to note that even though the office of shepherd is consigned to Peter, the text continues to speak of my sheep, that is, the sheep of Jesus. Peter is not being appointed "lord" of the sheep—they never can or will belong to him—but only the shepherd of Jesus' sheep. As a result, clear limits are set to Peter's office as shepherd.

What does this text say and what does it not say? It speaks of an exceptional position for Peter. At the level of our text we are dealing with John's interpretation of Peter and his role in the primitive Church. No one disputes today that the text does not give us authentic words of Jesus to Peter but rather words fashioned by the Johannine tradition. Even the well-known words about the rock in Matthew (16:17-19) are not authentic words of Jesus but a relatively late production of the community which receives its final touches from Matthew the evangelist and articulates a conception of Peter's role that is strongly Jewish-Christian in character.[174]

After the death and resurrection of Jesus Peter was the one who functioned as shepherd of the flock of Jesus; this is the concept the Johannine circle had of Peter. His role is one of service as deputy

150

shepherd and does not bring with it any domination or claims to power. In this sense there is no problem in speaking of a Petrine office, although not in the sense of a fixed institution, but rather in the sense of a leadership role that is linked to the person of Peter and motivated and sustained by his personal commitment, his unshakeable love for Jesus. It would be difficult to explain how unshakeable love for Jesus can be given institutional status.

Nor does the passage say anything about a successor to Peter. This strikes us all the more since the text goes on to speak of Peter's death. What is said is that Peter is called to serve as deputy shepherd for Jesus' sheep; nothing is said about who will replace Peter or even whether anyone is to replace him at all. Rather, in this passage nothing is decided on this point. It is impossible therefore to deduce from this and other passages on Peter in the New Testament a Petrine office along the lines of the Roman papacy with its primacy of jurisdiction and its conception of infallibility.

The primitive Church hardly thought of history as continuing for a lengthy period, and therefore it did not develop any hierarchic system of offices. Of course, as time went on, new needs inevitably arose, and to meet them new offices were developed (such as the monarchical episcopate and a primacy in the sense of an apex which symbolized unity). In turn, connections with the past were sought for these offices in order to preserve the historical continuity of the Church. But the New Testament period hardly provided any texts and binding rules which showed in detail the character these offices should have; in the beginning there were many possible ways of proceeding.

From the historian's point of view the actual development that took place is quite understandable. But I think that its absolutization is ill-founded. It is a mistake to think that because things *did* develop this way, therefore they *had* to develop this way, and that we cannot conceive of them being otherwise or change them in the slightest. According to this argument, the development that took place was willed by God and the Holy Spirit, and was in fact the only possible development. Not so. The development was not of divine but of human and ecclesiastical law. The present form of the Petrine office, as embodied in the pope of Rome, is not the only possible or conceivable form such an office might take; it is possible to give the Petrine office another form. According to the ecclesiology of John, a democratic, fraternal, and synodal constitution for the Church is quite conceivable. When all is said and done, any constitution for the Church is intelligible and possible that acknowledges the unconditional primacy of Jesus, who alone is the good shepherd of his sheep.

"And lead you where you do not wish to go" (vv. 18-19). This passage is evidently a prophecy formulated after the event; the event that has taken place is the death of Peter. The prophecy takes the form of an image in which youth and age are contrasted: young people make their own decisions about their lives; old people must allow others to gird them and lead them where they do not wish to go. This statement may have been a general proverb which the author is here taking over and, by the addition of a few words, applying to the violent death of Peter. The result is one of the very rare references in the New Testament to the death of Peter as a martyr. The essential point is the violence: others have taken control of Peter and led him where he did not want to go.

According to tradition Peter was executed in about A.D. 64 during Nero's persecution of the Christians. Legend says that he was crucified head downward. It is really cause for constant amazement that the deaths of the leading apostles and disciples of Jesus should have left so little trace in the New Testament writings, despite the fact that the writings, especially the gospels and the Acts of the Apostles, came into existence only after these deaths. Apparently the primitive Church did not overly regret the departure of these men.

Yet the reason for this attitude was not a lack of reverence for them. The reason is probably to be seen in the fact that faith in Jesus Christ gave people a new attitude to the basic human facts of death and life, an attitude quite different from that revealed by the customary funeral pomp of antiquity. A further factor was probably aversion to publicity.

When people were convinced, as the writer of John is, of the presence of new life through faith and love, then, as far as its meaning in the eyes of faith is concerned, death was in fact stripped of its power. The important thing was that the cause of Jesus was continuing. This is precisely why the final words which Jesus addresses to Peter and, beyond him, to all readers, are, "Follow me!" The continuity of living Christianity does not depend, in the last analysis, on persons, offices, and institutions; these have only a subordinate service function. It depends first and foremost on following Jesus.

THE BELOVED DISCIPLE (21:20–24); THE SECOND CONCLUDING REMARK (21:25)

The contrast between Peter and the beloved disciple in this passage is doubtless to be attributed to the author of the supplementary chapter. The author gives the impression that he actually knew such a disciple and therefore that he possesses the key to those passages of the gospel that speak of this disciple.

Apart from the supplementary chapter there are three such passages, as well as a couple of further references. The disciple is first introduced at the last supper, in 13:23-26: "One of the disciples, the one whom Jesus loved, was reclining on the bosom of Jesus." The description, "whom Jesus loved," is repeated in 19:26-27 and 20:20. For simplicity's sake we shall speak of him as the beloved disciple.

According to 19:26-27 he is the only disciple who stands beneath the cross; in a kind of testament Jesus commits his mother to this disciple's care. He also seems to be the one meant by the eyewitness of 19:35, whose testimony is presented as utterly reliable and credible. According to 20:2(-10) the beloved disciple runs with Peter to the tomb; in this passage he is also called the other disciple (20:3, 4, 8) who reaches the empty tomb before Peter and who attains to Easter faith.

We may also mention some other passages that have often been connected with the beloved disciple. In 1:35-40, where two disciples join Jesus after hearing what John the Baptist says of him, only one of them is named (Andrew), while the name of the other is omitted. In the past it was often surmised that this unnamed disciple is no other than the beloved disciple; 18:15-16 also speaks of another disciple: Peter and another disciple follow Jesus to the palace of the high priest. This other disciple is known to the high priest and therefore has no difficulty in entering the courtyard of the palace. Later he comes out and brings Peter back in with him. It is uncertain whether these two passages really refer to the beloved disciple. The connection made with the latter is based on the phrase "the [or:an] other disciple," which occurs in both passages. But the possibility that in all the passages mentioned we have to do with a literary figure whom the evangelist himself has introduced into the story for narrative purposes, must at least be taken into consideration.[175]

The only secure point of departure is the fact that the beloved disciple is a personage of the fourth gospel who comes on the scene in the contexts mentioned. He appears with Peter in 13:23-26 and 20:2-10; elsewhere he is an isolated figure. Literary reasons for his appearance might be: a mediatorial role, a testamentary concern of Jesus, a witness function, or even some symbolic intention. As a matter of fact, the view has repeatedly been put forth that the beloved disciple is a purely symbolic personage. The question which then arises is whether or not the figure of the beloved disciple can really be explained wholly in terms of the functions that have been mentioned. There must be specific reasons why he repeatedly appears alongside Peter and is evidently very close to or intimate with Jesus.

Clearly, we come closer to discerning these reasons when we take the supplementary chapter into account.[176] We have already seen that in 21:7 the beloved disciple has been introduced, at a later time, into an older tradition; the author must have had a special interest in him. He is the disciple who first recognizes Jesus: "It is the Lord." After this there is not a word more about him in the story. The concern of the author may be seen in the fact that he has introduced the figure of the beloved disciple into this story, in which, in all probability, it played no part originally, because it was especially important to him. Even in the Easter appearance in Galilee the beloved disciple has to be part of the scene, for here again he must be the first to recognize Jesus.

Verse 20 immediately makes a reference back to 13:23-26: "Peter turns around and sees the disciple whom Jesus loved following— the one who at the supper had reclined on Jesus' breast and had asked, 'Lord, who is the one who is betraying you?' " The author is here making an identification: the beloved disciple is the same one of whom the gospel has already spoken. In the present passage he follows Jesus. Especially in view of Jesus' final words to Peter, "Follow me," we must understand the words in their heightened theological sense; that is, the following of Jesus has the technical

154

meaning that it has elsewhere in the New Testament when describing the authentic disciple of Jesus. The meaning here, therefore, is, while Peter looks back and hesitates, the beloved disciple is already on the right path of the following of Jesus. He is thus the true disciple of Jesus, since following is the essence of discipleship.

At the same time, however, this passage manifests a special interest in the *person* of this disciple, an interest that surely goes beyond any purely functional understanding of him. The proof is that Peter asks about the further lot of this disciple: "Lord, what about him?" To this Jesus gives an enigmatic answer: "If I want him to remain until I come, what concern is it of yours. Follow me!" (vv. 21-22).

The answer of Jesus as formulated here is a rebuff; it is also an authoritative utterance. The further destiny of the beloved disciple is none of Peter's business! The question then arises, what is the meaning of this following?, and the answer to be given evidently is that there are various types of following. One way is that of Peter; by means of the violence done him by outsiders it leads him to martyrdom. But the other disciple, the beloved disciple, is no less a follower of Jesus. When Peter looks back at him, he sees him already following Jesus, and no more than this can be asked of him. It is no business of Peter where Jesus is leading this disciple or even if this other is not to die a martyr's death.

It is quite conceivable that in this passage the author wanted to resolve a dispute. Peter and certainly many other disciples as well had died a martyr's death, like Jesus himself. Beyond a doubt this gave them a high reputation as radical followers of Jesus who carried their crosses after him to the point of dying with him. Was not a martyr's death the authentic goal, the crown of victory, of a real disciple's life? But what if there were disciples of Jesus who had followed him from the first hour but who had reached old age and did not die a martyr's death? Or even Christian who were ready to spend their lives following Jesus but did not long wholeheartedly for martyrdom? The author's answer settles the issue here: Both ways of following are good ones. We must let Jesus decide which way he will lead the individual disciple, for the same way is not suited to all.

The answer also takes a position on the problem of the delay of the parousia. The words, "If I want him to remain until I come

155

. . . ," refer to the parousia. If Jesus wants to let the disciple live on until the parousia, he has the authority to do so. The statement doubtless exaggerates, but nonetheless it may at some point have gotten into circulation in Johannine circles as a saying about the beloved disciple. The older the beloved disciple grew, the more people may have said, "Jesus has preserved this man for himself, until he comes again! He is to see the parousia!" As verse 23 tells us, the saying gave rise to the misunderstanding that the beloved disciple was never to die; it was a misunderstanding that could last, of course, only during the lifetime of the disciple. Now the misunderstanding has been corrected, because in the meantime the beloved disciple has in fact died! This makes it possible to explain that Jesus had not in fact said, "The disciple will not die," but had merely suggested this as a possibility: "If I want him to remain until the parousia, what business is it of yours?" The words themselves and the correction of their misinterpretation hardly seem academic and purely literary. If, then, the text does allude to the death of the beloved disciple, it gives us a glimpse of historical fact. The beloved disciple is evidently not a mere figure out of literature; behind him there seems to be a historical personage.

In verse 24 the author makes a final identification of the beloved disciple: "This is the disciple who testifies to all this and has written it down, and we know that his testimony is true." In other words, for the author of the supplementary chapter, the beloved disciple is the key witness to the Johannine tradition (see also 19:35, to which explicit reference is probably being made here). He is also the author of the gospel. As thus interpreted, our text is the oldest witness to, and at the same time the oldest interpretation of, the beloved disciple as both the corroborator and the author of the gospel of John. This statement holds, of course, only if the author of chapter 21 is not also the author of the gospel. But if this suggestion is well-founded, the testimony of the author of chapter 21 becomes in turn the oldest regarding the gospel of John and its author. With a certain justification we can call him the first editor of the gospel of John. This, however, raises the important question of the purpose and credibility of the editor in making his statement.

The purpose of the editor in making his statement is undoubtedly to show that the beloved disciple is not a fictitious, symbolic figure but a historical person and specifically an eyewitness and the author of the gospel. This, of course, does not absolutely exclude the possibility that his statement is nonetheless a fiction; that is, that he is falsely ascribing the work to an author or engaging in some other form of mimicry. This would not be reason for automatically condemning his action, since, like the pseudonymous authors of the non-genuine Pauline letters, his concern would be for apostolic tradition and continuity, whatever he may have conceived this to be.

Toward the end of the first century evidence of genuine apostolic tradition had become an important criterion for early Christians. The editor of the gospel of John took up this concern and applied it for his own purposes. His thesis is that the author of the gospel was a genuine disciple whose testimony is true. For—according to him—the author is no other than the beloved disciple. Thus he also commends the gospel of John to the great Church. In the form of this gospel the beloved disciple thus becomes a key exponent of authentic early Christian tradition about Jesus. This is probably the most important thing that can be said about this personage.

Is the beloved disciple to be identified with the evangelist? According to the editor he is; of this there can be no doubt. He is the disciple who testifies to all this and has written it down. There are various ways of explaining this statement: the editor has the historical facts straight; or we are faced with a deliberate fiction or with an inadequate knowledge of the real history of the tradition; or, finally, the terms witness and author are to be taken in a broader sense.

R. Schnackenburg has recently turned his attention once again to this question: "Can we suppose that there is a historical person behind the disciple whom Jesus loved, and, if so, what kind of person was he?"[177]

> In the disciple whom Jesus loved we have the authority on which the Johannine circle relies, a disciple of the Lord, but one who was not among the "Twelve." His pupils and friends were interested in locating him in the circle of disciples closest to Jesus, because his tradition and his interpretation of the revelation given in and through Jesus was the basis of their own preaching and teaching and the foundation of the self-understanding of their community or communities. They regarded him as a reliable representative of tradition and even more as a Spirit-enlightened preacher

and interpreter of the message of Jesus and therefore as the ideal disciple of Jesus. . . . At a time when communities were reflecting more and more on the "apostolic" authorities who stood behind them, they were also interested in the normative witnesses they were following and in the traditions these represented. Therefore they collected the notes these men had made and their oral communications, their theological teachings and interpretations, and compiled these—probably in accordance with the master's own plan—into a gospel which they intended to use in their own communities and also to make known in the Church at large.

Not much more than this can be honestly asserted. The representatives of apostolic tradition in the second half of the first century were for the most part anonymous. We know only a few—perhaps even only one: Luke—by their true names. With this we must probably be content for all time to come.

As the synoptic gospels and the gospel of John show in their various ways, only the person of Jesus Christ proved to be the abiding basis of Christian continuity and identity. He alone is the true light that enlightens everyone, whether in the world at large or in the community of those who believe in him and, like Peter, love him more than all others.

NOTES

WORKS FREQUENTLY CITED

Blank, J. *Krisis: Untersuchungen zur johanneischen Christologie und Eschatologie* (Freiburg, 1964).
————. "Die Verhandlung vor Pilatus. Joh 18, 28-19, 16 im Lichte der johanneischer Theologie," *Biblische Zeitschrift* 3 (1959), pp. 60-81.
————. "The God of the Living" (i. The scandal of the cross; ii. Jesus' resurrection), in J. Feiner and L. Vischer (eds.), *The Common Catechism: A Book of Christian Faith*, tr. by D. Bourke et al. (New York, 1975), pp. 142-85.
Blinzler, J. *Der Prozess Jesu* (3rd ed.; Regensburg, 1960). A translation of the 2nd edition by I. McHugh and F. McHugh appeared earlier: *The Trial of Jesus* (Westminster, Md., 1959); the translation of quoted material which is already present in the 2nd edition will be taken from *The Trial of Jesus*.
Bultmann, R. *The Gospel of John: A Commentary*, tr. by G. R. Beasley-Murray, R. W. N. Hoare, and J. K. Riches (Philadelphia, 1971).
Dauer, A. *Die Passionsgeschichte im Johannesevangelium* (StANT 30; Munich, 1972; with bibliography).
Dodd, C. H. *Historical Tradition in the Fourth Gospel* (Cambridge, 1961).
Hahn, "Der Prozess Jesu nach dem Johannesevangelium," *EKK* 2 (1970), pp. 23-96.
Schlier, H. "Jesus und Pilatus nach dem Johannesevangelium," in his *Die Zeit der Kirche* (Freiburg, 1956), pp. 56-74 (=*Aufsätze zur biblischen Theologie* [Leipzig, 1968], pp. 262-80).
Schnackenburg, R. *Das Johannesevangelium* (Herders Theologischer Kommentar zum Neuen Testament 4), 3 vols. (Freiburg, 1965, 1971, 1975). English translation of vols. 1 and 2: *The Gospel according to St. John* (New York-London, 1968, 1979).
Schürmann, H. *Jesu ureigener Tod* (Freiburg, 1975).
Winter, P. *On The Trial of Jesus* (2nd ed.; New York, 1974).

BHWH *Biblisch-historisches Handwörterbuch*. Ed. by B. Reicke and L. Rost (Göttingen, 1962-66).

LTK² *Lexicon für Theologie und Kirche*. New ed. by J. Höfer and K. Rahner (Freiburg, 1957-65).

TDNT *Theological Dictionary of the New Testament*. Ed. by G. Kittel, tr. by G. Bromiley (Grand Rapids, 1964-74).

NOTES

1 Friedrich Nietzsche, *The Anti-Christ*, no. 35, tr. by R. J. Hollingdale (Baltimore, 1968), pp. 147-48.

2 Dodd, p. 29.

3 Dauer, p. 336.

4 Cf. Dauer, passim; Hahn, pp. 25, 33, 54.

5 *Jewish War* I, 98; *Antiquities of the Jews* XIII, 380.

6 *Jewish War* II, 78; *Antiquities* XVII, 295. Cf. also *Jewish War* II, 241, 253; *Antiquities* XX, 129.

7 On this point cf. W. Grundmann, F. Hesse, M. de Jonge, and A. S. van der Woude, "chriō," *TDNT* 9:493-580, and especially W. Grundmann, "The Christ-Statements of the New Testament," pp. 327-73.

8 Cf. *Jewish War* II, 55-65.

9 Grundmann, "chriō," pp. 537-38.

10 Ibid., p. 528.

11 Recently by Pinchas E. Lapide, *Der Rabbi von Nazareth: Wandlungen des jüdischen Jesusbildes* (Trier, 1974).

12 Ibid., p. 39.

13 Cf. Matt. 11:2 = Luke 7:19 (Q); Mark 6:17-19 = Matt. 14:3-12.

14 Mark 6:14-16 par., with Matt. 14:1-2; Luke 9:7-9

15 Josephus, *Antiquities* XVIII, 118-19.

16 Karl-Heinz Müller, "Jesus und die Sadduzäer," in *Biblische Randbemerkungen: Schülerfestschrift für R. Schnackenburg* (Würzburg, 1974), pp. 3-24.

17 Ibid., p. 3.

18 Ibid., p. 18.

19 *Jewish War* VI, 300-5, tr. by G. A. Williamson, *Josephus: The Jewish War* (Baltimore, 1959), pp. 349-50.

20 "Jesus und die Sadduzäer," Müller, p. 17.

21 Ibid., pp. 28-29.

22 Ibid., p. 30.

23 Ibid., p. 31.

24 Ibid.

25 Ibid.

26 Ibid., pp. 32-33.

27 Hahn, p. 86; cf. also Blank, *Krisis*, pp. 246 ff.

28 Schlier, p. 56.

29 Bultmann, pp. 209-10.

30 Schnackenburg, 2:6 ff.

31 See the discussion in Schnackenburg, 2:396.

32 Ibid., p. 396.

33 Cf. Hahn, p. 25.

34 The Pharisees in John: 1:24; 3:1; 4:1; 7:32, 45, 47, 48; 8:13; 9:13, 15, 16, 40; 11:46, 47, 57; 12:19, 42; 18:3.

35 Schnackenburg, 2:448.

36 Machiavelli, *The Prince,* chap. 17, tr. by A. Gilbert, *Machiavelli: The Chief Works and Others* (Durham, N.C., 1965), 1:61-62.

37 C. K. Barrett, *The Gospel according to John* (London, 1955), pp. 338-39; Schnackenburg, 2:449.

38 R. Meyer, "prophētēs," *TDNT* 6:825.

39 *Antiquities* XIII, 299; cf. *Jewish War* I. 68.

40 Cf. Mark 14:32-43, 43-52 par., with Matt. 26:36-46, 47-56; Luke 22:39-46, 47-53.

41 Cf. K. Kundsin, *Topologische Überlieferungsstoffe im Johannes-Evangelium* (Göttingen, 1925).

42 Josephus, *Jewish War* III, 67.

43 J. Jeremias, *Jerusalem in the Time of Jesus*, tr. by F. H. and C. H. Cave (Philadelphia, 1969), p. 210.

44 Cf. ibid.

45 Irenaeus, *Adversus haereses* I, 26, 1, tr. in R. M. Grant (ed.), *Gnosticism: A Source Book of Heretical Writings from the Early Christian Period* (New York, 1961), p. 41 (italics added).

46 Cf. Mark 14:47; Matt. 26:51-54; Luke 22:50-51.

47 Cf. the presentations of Blinzler and Winter.

48 Josephus, *Jewish War* II, 117 (Williamson, p. 125).

49 Cf. Bo Reicke, *The World of the Bible from 500 B.C. to A.D. 100*, tr. by D. E. Green (Philadelphia, 1968), pp. 142-52.

50 Ibid., pp. 142-43.

51 *Antiquities* XX, 195-99.

52 Cf. 2:14, 15; 5:14; 7:14, 28; 8:20, 59; 10:23.

53 Josephus, *Jewish War* VI, 303 (Williamson, pp. 349-50).

54 Müller, "Jesus und die Sadduzäer," p. 17; cf. the citation above on n. 22.

55 On the entire problem cf. G. Schneider, *Verleugnung, Verspottung und Verhör Jesu nach Lukas 22, 54-71: Studien zur lukanischen Deutung der Passion* (StANT 22; Munich, 1969).

56 Cf. Blinzler, *Prozess*, pp. 205-19; *Trial*, pp. 194-204.

57 *Prozess*, p. 211; *Trial*, p. 203

58 *Prozess*, p. 219.

59 Cf. Luke 3:1, 19; 8:3, 9; 7:9; 13:31; 23:7, 8, 11, 12, 15; Acts 4:27.

60 Cf. Blinzler, *Prozess*, p. 224; *Trial*, p. 209.

61 Verse 17, which is lacking in some important mss, must therefore have been a later addition.

62 *Prozess*, pp. 232-34; *Trial*, pp. 218-21.

63 Tractate Pesahim 8, 6a, tr. in Blinzler, *Trial*, p. 219.

64 Ibid.

65 M. Dibelius, *Jesus*, tr. by C. B. Hedrick and F. C. Grant (Philadelphia, 1959).

66 Ibid.

67 Philo, *Against Flaccus* 36-39, tr. by F. H. Colson, *Philo* 9 (Cambridge, Mass., 1960), pp. 323-325.

68 On this cf. Blinzler, *Prozess*, pp. 187-98; *Trial*, pp. 177-84; E. Schürer, *A History of the Jewish People in the Time of Jesus Christ*, tr. by J. Macpherson (Edinburgh, 1885-91), First Division, 1:82-89; *BHHW* 3:1472-73.

69 Philo, *Embassy to Gaius* 301-2, tr. by F. H. Colson, *Philo* 10 (Cambridge, Mass., 1962), pp. 151, 153.

70 Josephus, *Jewish War*, II, 169-74; *Antiquities* XVIII, 55-59.

71 Josephus, *Jewish War*, II, 175-77; *Antiquities* XVIII, 60-62.

72 Josephus, *Antiquities* XVIII, 88-89.

73 Schürer, *History*, First Division, 1:87, n. 139.

74 Josephus, *Jewish War* V, 238 (Williamson, p. 295).

75 Josephus, *Jewish War* V, 243-45 (Williamson, p. 295); cf. "Prätorium," *BHHW* 3:1482.

76 Josephus, *Jewish War* VI, 426-27 (Williamson, p. 359).

77 Bultmann, p. 651, n. 6.

78 Schlier, p. 88.

79 Ibid., p. 59

80 F. Hesse, "chriō," *TDNT* 9:498.

81 1 QS IX, 11; Dan. 12:34-35; 14:19; 20:1; etc.

82 O. Cullmann, *The Christology of the New Testament*, tr. by S. C. Guthrie and C. A. M. Hall (rev. ed.; Philadelphia, 1963), p. 113.

83 Thus Pinchas Lapide, *Der Rabbi von Nazareth*, pp. 33-35.

84 Schlier, p. 64.

85 This commentary has insisted on a number of occasions that the evangelist uses the term "the Jews" in a schematic way and generalizes it to mean "worldly" existence and ways of acting. We call attention to this point once again here lest John be misunderstood as referring to the Jews who were living at that time or to the Jewish people as a whole. This must be kept in mind with regard to all the texts in which the expression occurs. In addition, we have indicated in connection with several passages that historically it was the leaders among the Sadducees, a class comprising the priests and the aristocracy, who were responsible for the condemnation of Jesus.

86 On this cf. also 5:41-47, especially v. 43; 10:1, 8, 10, 12.

87 Thomas Aquinas, *Commentaria in Evangelium Joannis*, nos. 2373-78.

88 Bultmann, p. 659.

89 Ibid.

90 Josephus, *Antiquities* XX, 199; cf. also Schürer, *History*, Second Division, 2:36-37.

91 For a discussion of this problem in the literature, cf. especially Blinzler, *Prozess*, pp. 11-28; *Trial*, pp. 22-48.

92 Cf. G. Stählin, "phileō," *TDNT* 9:166-67; A. N. Sherwin-White, *Roman Society and Roman Law in the New Testament* (Oxford, 1963), pp. 46-47.

93 Blinzler, *Prozess*, p. 249; *Trial*, p. 236.

94 Sherwin-White, *Roman Society*, p. 47.

95 Cf. D. H. Wallace, "Gabbatha," *BHHW* 1:506-7.

96 Quoted by H.-W. Kuhn, "Jesus als Gekreuzigter in der frühchristlichen Verkündigung bis zur Mitte des 2. Jahrhunderts," *Zeitschrift für katholische Theologie* 72 (1975), pp. 7-8.

97 Ibid., pp. 8-9.

98 The passage is probably constructed in imitation of Luke 21:20-24 where Luke is likewise alluding to the subsequent destruction of Jerusalem.

99 Eusebius, *Historia ecclesiastica* III, 5, 6, tr. by G. Williamson, *Eusebius: The History of the Church* (Baltimore, 1965), p. 112.

100 G. Dalman, *Orte und Wege Jesu* (Gütersloh, 1919; 3rd. ed., 1924; reprinted: Darmstadt, 1967), p. 365.

101 W. F. Eltester, "Golgotha," *BHHW* 1:584; cf. G. Kopp, "Golgotha," *LTK* 4:1046-47.

102 Blinzler, *Prozess*, p. 269; *Trial*, pp. 252-53.

103 Blinzler, *Prozess*, p. 271; *Trial*, p. 255.

104 Blinzler, *Prozess*, p. 270, n. 36; *Trial*, p. 254, n. 34.

105 Cf. especially Kuhn, "Jesus als Gekreuzigter," p. 5, n. 13.

106 Blinzler, *Prozess*, p. 271, *Trial*, pp. 254-55, defends the historicity but the arguments he offers are hardly persuasive.

107 This is a fault that affects Blinzler's entire portrayal of the trial of Jesus.

108 [A *crux gemmata* is a cross adorned with gems and precious stones.]

109 Dauer, p. 316.

110 For the whole problem cf. especially Dauer, pp. 196-201, 318-33; H. Schürmann, "Jesu letzte Weisung. Joh. 19, 26-27," in *Sapienter ordinare (Festschrift für E. Kleineidam)* (Leipzig, 1969), pp. 105-23 (reprinted in Schürmann's *Ursprung und Gestalt* [Düsseldorf, 1970], pp. 13-28).

111 Cf. Dauer, pp. 196 ff.

112 Dauer, p. 200

113 Schürmann, *Ursprung und Gestalt*, p. 14.

114 Cf. also Prov. 23:22; 30:17; Sir. 3:16; 4:10.

115 Dauer, p. 322.

116 *Commentaria in Evangelium Joannis*, no. 2441.

117 Bultmann, p. 673.

118 Schürmann, *Ursprung und Gestalt*, p. 16.

119 Ibid., p. 25; cf. Dauer, pp. 329 ff.

120 E. C. Hoskyns, *The Fourth Gospel*, ed. by F. N. Davey (London, 1947), p. 530.

121 Bultmann, p. 675.

122 Josephus, *Jewish War* IV, 330 (Williamson, p. 248).

123 Cf. Blinzler, *Prozess*, p. 287.

124 Ibid.

125 Augustine, *In Evangelium Joannis tractatus* 120, 2 (*CCL* 36:661).

126 On this point cf. Blank, *Krisis*, pp. 198 ff.

127 Cf. also Num. 9:12. Ps. 34:21 says of the "just man": "He [Yahweh] protects each of his limbs; not one of them shall be broken," but as read in the LXX this text does not figure as a source.

128 Cf. T. H. Robinson and F. Horst, *Die zwölf kleinen Propheten* (HAT 14; Tübingen, 1954), p. 255.

129 Ibid., pp. 256-57.

130 Cf. especially I. Broer, *Die Urgemeinde und das Grab Jesu: Eine Analyse der Grablegungsgeschichte im Neuen Testament* (StANT 31; Munich, 1972).

131 Cf. Blinzler, *Prozess*, pp. 289-99.

132 For a different view cf. Blinzler, *Prozess*, p. 287.

133 Cf. H. W. Strack and P. Billerbeck, *Kommentar zum Neuen Testament aus Talmud und Misrasch* 2 (Munich, 1924), pp. 52-53.

134 A selection of literature: R. Bultmann, "New Testament and Mythology: The Mythological Element in the Message of the New Testament and the Problem of Its Reinterpretation," in R. Bultmann et al., *Kerygma and Myth: A Theological Debate,* ed. by H. M. Bartsch and tr. by R. H. Fuller (London, 1953; references will be to Harper Torchbook ed. of 1961), pp. 1-44. Idem, *Theology of the New Testament,* tr. by K. Grobel (2 vols.; New York, 1951, 1955). Idem, "The Primitive Christian Kerygma and the Historical Jesus," in *The Historical Jesus and the Kerygmatic Christ,* ed. and tr. by C. E. Braaten and R. A. Harrisville (New York & Nashville, 1964), pp. 15-42. J. Blank, *Paulus und Jesus* (StANT 18; Munich, 1968). Idem, "The God of the Living," in J. Feiner and L. Vischer (eds.), *The Common Catechism: A Book of Christian Faith,* tr. by D. Bourke et al., pp. 142-85. E. Schillebeeckx, *Jesus: An Experiment in Christology,* tr. by H. Hoskins (New York, 1979). R. Mahoney, *Two Disciples at the Tomb: The Background and Message of John 20, 1-10* (Bern & Frankfurt, 1974).

135 Schillebeeckx, *Jesus,* p. 331.

136 Bultmann, *Theology,* 1:42-43.

137 Schillebeeckx, *Jesus,* p. 387.

138 Ibid., p. 294.

139 Ibid., pp. 311-12.

140 Ibid., p. 393.

141 Blank, "The God of the Living," p. 158.

142 Bultmann, "New Testament and Mythology," p. 39.

143 Ibid., p. 42.

144 Schillebeeckx, *Jesus*, p. 346.

145 Cf. I. T. Ramsey, *Christian Discourse: Some Logical Explorations* (New York, 1965); cf. W. A. de Pater, *Theologische Sprachlogik* (Munich, 1971).

146 Ramsey, *Christian Discourse*, pp. 79 ff.

147 de Pater, *Theologische Sprachlogik*, p. 48.

148 Schillebeeckx, *Jesus*, pp. 379-97.

149 Ibid., p. 390.

150 Bultmann, "New Testament and Mythology," p. 42.

151 This third view, which has been argued especially by K. Lehmann, *Auferweckt am dritten Tag nach der Schrift* (Quaestiones Disputatae 38; Freiburg i. Br., 1968), seems to me today more probable than the view I adopted in my book *Paulus und Jesus:* "The words 'on the third day' give a date that agrees with the primitive Christian tradition reflected in the gospels and refers to the discovery of the empty tomb" (p. 156), although in the gospels the "chronological understanding" of the words is undoubtedly primary.

152 Cf. Gen. 12:7; 17:1; 18:1; 26:1; 35:1-9; 48:3; Exod. 3:2, 16; 4:1, 5; 6:3.

153 Cf. Matt. 28:16; Luke 24:9, 33; Acts 1:28; 2:14.

154 It is clear that the connection between Mark 16:7 and 14:27-28 is due to the redactional work of the evangelist.

155 Bultmann, *John*, p. 681.

156 20:2, 13, 15, 18, 20, 25, 28; 21:7, 12, 15, 16, 17, 20, 21.

157 Cf. 7:38; 13:18; 17:12; 19:24, 28, 36, 37.

158 Bultmann, *John*, p. 685.

159 R. Mahoney, in his perceptive study of John 20:1-10, *Two Disciples at the Tomb*.

160 Ibid., p. 278.

161 H. von Campenhausen, "The Events of Easter and the Empty Tomb," in his *Tradition and Life in the Church: Essays and Lectures in Church History,* tr. by A. V. Littledale (Philadelphia, 1968), p. 66.

162 G. Söhngen, in *Deutsche Thomas-Ausgabe* 6 (Salzburg, 1937), p. 431, n. 47.

163 Cf. Matt. 10:3; Mark 3:18; Luke 6:15; Acts 1:13.

164 Cf. Flavius Philostratus, *Vita Apollonii.*

165 On the various problems cf. W. G. Kümmel, *Introduction to the New Testament,* tr. from the 19th German ed. by H. C. Kee (Nashville, 1975), pp. 234-46; A. Wikenhauser, *Einleitung in das Neue Testament,* 6th ed. by J. Schmid (Freiburg, 1973), pp. 323-45; Bultmann, *John,* pp. 700 ff.; Schnackenburg, "Der Jünger, den Jesus liebte," *EKK* 2 (1970), pp. 97-117.

166 Cf. Kümmel, *Introduction,* pp. 207-8, and Schnackenburg, *John* 1:73: "The redactors are certainly responsible for ch. 21, where they may have used material from the evangelist," as in the story of the great catch of fish; cf. now Schnackenburg, *Johannes* 3:415 ff.

167 A. Schlatter, *Der Evangelist Johannes* (3rd ed.; Stuttgart, 1960), p. 363.

168 On this passage cf. R. Pesch, *Der reiche Fischfang Lk 5, 1-11/Joh 21, 1-14: Wundergeschichte-Berufungserzählung-Erscheinungsbericht* (Düsseldorf, 1969).

169 Thus M. Dibelius, *From Tradition to Gospel,* tr. by B. L. Woolf (New York, 1919), p. 113; for a different interpretation cf. Bultmann, *John,* p. 705.

170 Cf. 6:9: "There is a boy here who has five barley loaves and two fishes"; also Mark 6:38; Matt. 14:17; Luke 9:13; cf. also Matt. 15:34.

171 Cf. Augustine, *In Evangelium Joannis tractatus* 122, 8 (*CCL* 36:673): "If you add 2 to 1, 3 is the result; if to this you add 3 and 4, the total is 10. If you then add the following numbers up to 17, the sum total is the number given in the text [i.e. 153]." 1 + 2 + 3 + 4 . . . + 17 = 153. Conclusion: the number 153 is meant to symbolize the totality of the elect: "This number, therefore, symbolizes, that is, signifies in a symbolic way, all who belong to this grace [the Spirit]."

172 On the Petrine problem cf. J. Blank, "The Person and Office of Peter in the New Testament," in E. Schillebeeckx and B. van Iersel (eds.), *Truth and Certainty* (Concilium 83; New York, 1973), pp. 42-55, with further bibliography.

173 Schnackenburg, *Johannes* 2:110.

174 Cf. Blank, "The Person and Office of Peter," pp. 50-52.

175 Cf. Mahoney, *Two Disciples*, pp. 281 ff., and the present commentary.

176 Cf. Mahoney, *Two Disciples*, pp. 286-301.

177 Schnackenburg, "Der Jünger, den Jesus liebte," pp. 109-10.